To John Stevens

xmas '83

W.W.II Hx

good reading

THE DEFENSE OF THE REICH

HITLER'S NIGHTFIGHTER PLANES AND PILOTS

WERNER HELD AND HOLGER NAUROTH

Translated by David Roberts

Arco Publishing, Inc. New York

Illustration credits: Falck 37, Jabs 55, Nacke 15, Bundesarchiv 69, Imperial War Museum 3, AMF 1, Holz 10, Diener 60, Dombrowsky 6, via Aders 27, Drewes 9, Rumpelhardt 10, Fengler 26, Scholl 21, USAF 1, Nonnenmacher 8, Dornier 11, Fuerst 8, Rökker 6, Lorant 1, Crow 1, Authors' Collection 127; plus two drawings by Bob Lasly.
Additional sources: Aders, *Geschichte der deutschen Nachtjagd;* Bekker, *Angriffshöhe 4000;* Obermaier, *Die Ritterkreuzträger der Luftwaffe.*

Published in 1982 by
Arco Publishing, Inc.
219 Park Avenue South, New York, N.Y. 10003

First German-language edition *Diè deutsche Nachtjagd*
© Motorbuch Verlag, Postfach 1370, 7000 Stuttgart
First English-language edition © Lionel Leventhal Limited, 1982

Library of Congress Cataloging in Publication Data
Main entry under title:

Defense of the Reich.

 Translation of Die Deutsche Nachtjagd.
 1. World War, 1939–45—Aerial operations, German—Pictorial Works. 2. Night fighter planes—Pictorial works. 3. World War, 1939–45—Germany—Pictorial works. 4. Germany—History—1933–1945—Pictorial Works. I. Held, Werner. II. Nauroth, Holger. III. Title: Defense of the Reich.
D787.D4713   940.54′4943   81–14925

ISBN 0–668–05393–3   AACR2

Printed in Great Britain.

Contents

Preface

When we began compiling this pictorial volume, the peculiarities connected with the theme of nightfighting were clear in our minds. A prime difficulty lay in that we needed to use photographs showing the special conditions involved in night combat; but the night, the natural element of the nightfighter, allows little in the way of photography, with the result that the procurement of suitable photographs was not easy, especially of those conveying the atmosphere of nightfighting. This book is neither a detailed chronicle nor a treatise on technical development; it is intended rather to enable the reader to form a vivid impression of the nightfighter's trade. With the help of these pictures, one can imagine in part the specialized conditions and requirements to which night combatants were subject. Artists' impressions help to clarify certain situations in which photography was impracticable. Interviews with numerous for-

mer members of the nightfighter service have produced a great deal of information, reports, suggestions and photographs, all of which are combined in this book.

We are deeply indebted to the following gentlemen, who helped in the preparation of this book: Oberst Wolfgang Falck (retd.), Kommodore NJG 1; Oberstleutnant Hans-Joachim Jabs (retd.), Kommodore NJG 1; Major Martin Drewes (retd.), III/NJG 1; Major Heinz Nacke (retd.), Kommandeur II/NJG 1; Messrs. Rumpelhardt, Diener, Aders, Dombrowsky, Holz, Fengler, Scholz and Nonnenmacher. We should also like to thank the Dornier company of Munich, the Bundesarchiv in Koblenz, the United States Air Force, Washington, the Imperial War Museum, London, and the AMF, Dübendorf, for their enthusiastic support.

Werner Held and Holger Nauroth

In the Beginning

The First World War saw the first successful attempts at nightfighting. Unfortunately, these successes were forgotten once the war ended, and the knowledge and experience resulting from them were lost. In 1936–37 some simple experiments in night combat took place; the results were not very promising, but the whole attempt had been rather haphazard and lacking the spur of necessity.

Nothing changed until April 1940, when Hauptmann Falck, the commander of I./ZG 1 based on the captured Danish airfield of Aalborg, decided to try an experiment of his own. He had been pondering for some time the question of how to intercept the RAF bombers that flew over every evening, and placed a few crews on standing alert. Thus one evening Hauptmann Falck, Oberleutnants Radusch and Streib, and Oberfeldwebel Thier lay in wait for the British. They were completely on their own, for at that time there was no ground control to help

them. Streib and Thier eventually made contact with the enemy, but Streib was unable to see the British aircraft clearly. Oberfeldwebel Thier, flying his Bf 110 well above the clouds, saw the British formation against the moonlit background, but lost them before he could get within firing range. Despite the lack of concrete results, the crews were further forward by one sighting, and a step closer to their goal. At the beginning of May, Wolfgang Falck was able to present his findings and suggestions to Udet, Milch and Kesselring; they fell on fertile ground. On 26 June 1940, after the end of the French campaign, Falck found himself in the presence of Göring, Kesselring (Luftflotte chief), Kästner (Head of Personnel) and Udet (General in charge of aircraft procurement). Possibly the most important outcome of this audience was the establishment, at Göring's behest, of the first nightfighter Geschwader. The Reichsmarschall appointed a startled Falck as Kommodore of NJG 1. The build-up phase was exceptionally difficult, for neither specialized aircraft nor crews trained for this new enterprise were available, and of organization the less said the better. The first Nachtjagddivision was established on 19 July 1940, under the leadership of Oberst Kammhuber. However, the experimental period was not yet over. On 20 July 1940, after numerous unsuccessful attempts, Oberleutnant Werner Streib scored the first victory for 'Helle Nachtjagd' or illuminated nightfighting. He and his colleagues were to have many more successes, but not before a lot of difficulties were overcome and a lot of sceptics convinced.

Many of the young, hitherto successful, Zerstörer (Bf 110) pilots took to this new type of fighting with little enthusiasm. Even the future ace Helmet Lent, discouraged after a few fruitless weeks, expressed a wish to get back to his old Zerstörer unit, and Falck, now a Major, had a hard task persuading him to stay on. But the way was prepared, and a new branch of the service was about to prove itself.

Above and left: Aalborg airfield, Denmark, the base of the Bf 110-equipped I./ZG 1, which became the nucleus of the German nightfighter arm. The first dusk fighter sorties were flown from here in the spring of 1940.

9

Left: Hauptmann Wolfgang Falck, Kommandeur of I./ZG 1, instigated the first dusk fighter flights, and thus may be considered the father of German nightfighting in World War Two.

Below: This Vickers Wellington of 149 Squadron, RAF, was claimed to be the first machine shot down on a night mission, by Oberleutnant Streib.

Before the Western campaign began, I./ZG 1 transferred to Kirschhellen, from where they took part in the invasion of France. Immediately after this campaign, Göring appointed Hauptmann Falck Kommodore of the newly established NJG 1.
Above: Kesselring, shortly before his promotion to General-feldmarschall, arrives at Kirschhellen.
Below: Hauptmann Falck accompanies the Feldmarschall on his tour of inspection of what would be (although nobody knew it at the time) I./NJG 1.
Right: Gruppenkommandeur Falck says goodbye to Kesselring in front of Falck's Bf 110C.

Above: A rare shot, taken during a night flight; the fighters are working in conjunction with searchlight batteries, whose light here illuminates the cockpit.
Left: The nightfighters' new emblem, designed by Hauptmann Falck, first appeared on this Bf 110C.
Below: An all-black Bf 110C nightfighter on a ferry flight.

Wolfgang Falck, now a Major, returns from a sortie (top) to a friendly greeting from the unit's long-haired Dachshund mascot (below).

The Bf 110, which did not fulfil expectations as a long-range day fighter, became the mainstay of the nightfighter arm, remaining in service in successive versions until the end of the war.

14

Top: In this propaganda photograph, a Heinkel 100 has been painted in a spurious nightfighter finish; in fact, few of this type were built, and they were used only by day in a Werksstaffel to protect the Heinkel factory.

Middle: A young Leutnant Lent displays the four victories he gained as a Zerstörer pilot. Two of the bars represent victories in the battle over the German Bight.

Below: Another founder member was Hauptmann Ehle, pictured here with radio operator Weng. Ehle, the second pilot to score a night victory, was appointed Kommandeur of II./NJG 1 in October 1940. The first two victories marked on the fin of his Bf 110 are Polish and the remainder British, the last six being night victories.

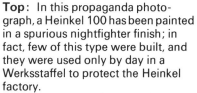

15

Left, top: It was rare for more than two nightfighters to
operate together.
Left, below: The wreck of a Vickers Wellington.
Above: A Bf 110 back on the ground after a successful sortie.

Above: 6 October 1940—Reichsmarschall Göring distributes Knights' Crosses to the first successful nightfighters. Second from left is Major Falck, sixth from left Oberleutnant Streib.
Left: Streib, the first pilot to shoot down an aircraft at night during World War Two, receives his Ritterkreuz from Luftwaffe Commander-in-Chief Hermann Göring.
Below: Major Falck, instigator of the first nightfighting trials, has his Knights' Cross put on him by a colleague.

Top: Repairs to Kommodore Major Falck's aircraft, damaged in action.
Middle: Falck prepares for take-off. Note the Geschwaderkommodore's standard on the car's mudguard.
Below: Arnheim, 1940. A Bf 110 of 4./NJG 1 at the end of the runway, awaiting the signal to take off.

Schematic representation of a night combat. A, visual contact; the German aircraft has just crossed the track of the British bomber. B, the Bf 110 has turned in to follow its opponent, and closes the range. C, the German fighter passes beneath the turning Lancaster and then climbs above it. D, the fighter flies a sweeping curve to bring it into firing position.

20

Above: Armourers work tirelessly to keep the guns in good working order.
Right: A routine but important task for the engine mechanics was checking engine revs against propeller pitch settings, as here on a Bf 110 of I./NJG 1.
Below: After repairs the aircraft and its equipment are tested in flight.

Top: The nightly briefing session at Leuwarden.
Middle: The first aircraft of the Staffel are prepared for take-off.
Below: A Do 17 Kauz follows a Bf 110 of II./NJG 1 out to the runway at Leuwarden.

22

Top: Hauptmann Streib, Kommandeur of 2./NJG 1, examining the guns of a Wellington he had shot down the previous night.
Below left: The wreckage of enemy bombers provided welcome raw material for the German aircraft industry.
Below right: RAF bomber crews join their Army comrades on morning roll-call in a POW camp.

Left: Leutnant Wolfgang Schnaufer, at the time a newcomer to nightfighting, boards his Bf 110.
Right: He prepares for his first operational sortie. He went on to become the top nightfighter ace.
Below: A Bf 110 takes off at night.

Top: Two 110s of 7./NJG 4, spring 1941.
Middle: Hauptmanns Streib and Nacke relax over coffee in Stade.
Below: The Flieger-HJ (air branch of the Hitler Youth) named a training glider after Heinrich Nacke. Even on such a rickety craft, the pilot looks determined to enjoy his first flight.

Top: A drawing by Hans Liska of a Bf 110 at readiness while another takes off. This sketch was published in *Signal* magazine.
Middle: Geschwader leader Major Falck, visiting Hauptmann Streib's Gruppe, watches an aircraft take off.
Below: Pioneers of nightfighting; left to right, Oberleutnant Eckardt, Hauptmann Nacke, Hauptmann Streib and Hauptmann Radusch.

Opposite page, top: Trainee radio operators learn air gunnery with the aid of a model Wellington.
Opposite page, below: A Ju 52 flying classroom from the Bordfunkerschule (Airborne Radio Operators' School) at Halle.

Left: The newcomer's knowledge is put to the test on his first flight in a Bf 110.
Below: Heinz Rökker in the He 51 which served as a trainer at the Nachtjagdvorschule (Elementary Nightfighter Training School) at Neubiberg in 1941. This aircraft carried all-black nightfighter camouflage.

Top left: Hauptmann Hans-Joachim Jabs, already a successful Zerstörer pilot, transferred to nightfighters in September 1941, and rose to become one of that service's outstanding personalities.
Top right: Martin Drewes entered the nightfighting arm at the end of 1941; he too went on to become a highly successful pilot.
Below: Oberleutnant Drewes in animated conversation with Feldwebel Erich Weissflog, radio operator to Hans-Joachim Jabs.

Above: Oberleutnant Eckart-Wilhelm von Bonin seen from the radio operator's position during preparations for take-off.
Left: Oberleutnant von Bonin (right) discusses a mission with his crew. He flew with II./NJG 1 from 1941, and was appointed commander of that Gruppe in 1943.
Below: Oberleutnant von Bonin 'bagged' this Wellington of 115 Squadron, RAF, which landed without further damage at Bonin's base.

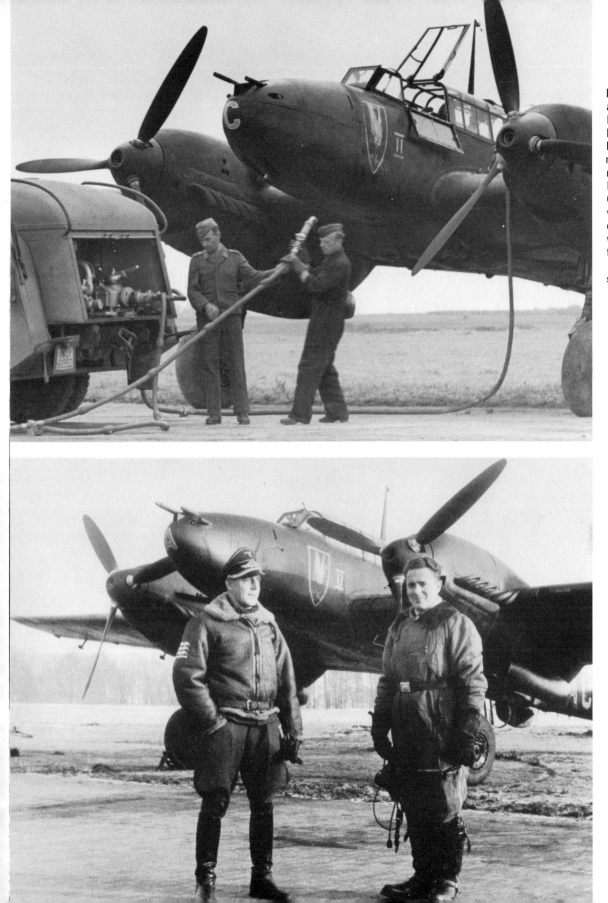

Left: Refuelling a Bf 110 of II./NJG 1 at Deelen, autumn 1940.
Below: Hauptmann Ehle, Kommandeur of II./NJG 1 from October 1940, with his radio operator, Oberfeldwebel Weng, in front of their Bf 110 just before a sortie.

Helle Nachtjagd: Nightfighting by Searchlight

By the beginning of 1941 the nightfighter arm was fully manned, organized and equipped for action. It stretched from Hamburg to the vicinity of Lüttich, but its line of searchlight coverage was subsequently extended as far as Flensburg in the north and Reims in the south. The defensive belt was initially divided into 18 sections, each 45 km (30 miles) wide and 35 km (20 miles) deep. Each section had a searchlight detachment, three aircraft and a communications company. The system worked as follows. A Freya radar station was set up ahead of the section to detect and range incoming raids. Four Würzburg radars then took over and tracked enemy aircraft, passing their information to the searchlight batteries via the local control room. The searchlights then illuminated the raiders for the fighters. Of the section's three Bf 110s one was already airborne, the second at readiness and the third was held in reserve. Later the organization was consolidated by the amalgamation of the sections into larger zones and the creation of associated Dunkelnachtjagd (Dark nightfighting) zones. The British, who had by now worked out the German tactics, took to diving through the illuminated areas, or else flying around them. In the first case the fighters could not engage before the bombers had left the illuminated zone, and in the second they never made contact. Thus the number of successful interceptions fell, giving a poor return for the massive technical and personnel investment. After June 1941, although Helle Nachtjagd (illuminated nightfighting) was still registering victories, the system was abandoned. A further reason for this discontinuation was that Hitler's Gauleiters (District Party Leaders), seeing the system's dwindling successes, demanded that the searchlights be sent back to assist the flak defences around major towns.

Opposite page: Frequent ferry flights became necessary as bases were shifted about. The Bf 110 in the top photograph is from II./NJG 1.

Josef Kammhuber estab-
lished the first Jagddivision in June 1940. Fresh
from French captivity, he
built up the nightfighter
arm and until 1943 led
the XIIth Fliegerkorps
(Flying Corps), which in-
corporated all the night
defence units. He was
Inspector of Nightfighters
until November 1943. An
altercation with the High
Command led to his re-
moval from home def-
ence, whereupon he was
posted to command Luft-
flotte (Air Fleet) 5 in
Norway.

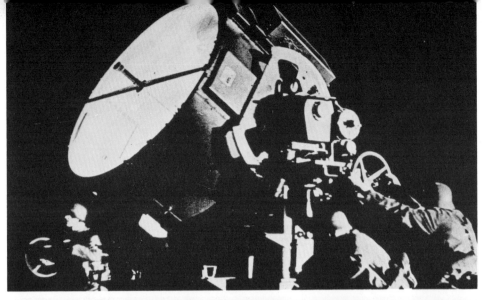

Top: A flak searchlight is trained on the approaching enemy.
Middle: Searchlight beams sweep the sky in search of the British bombers.
Below: Above the city, illuminated by searchlights, flares and fires, a nightfighter stalks a British bomber. (Translator's note: The Propaganda Korps artist whose impression this was evidently thought B-17s were in use as night bombers!)

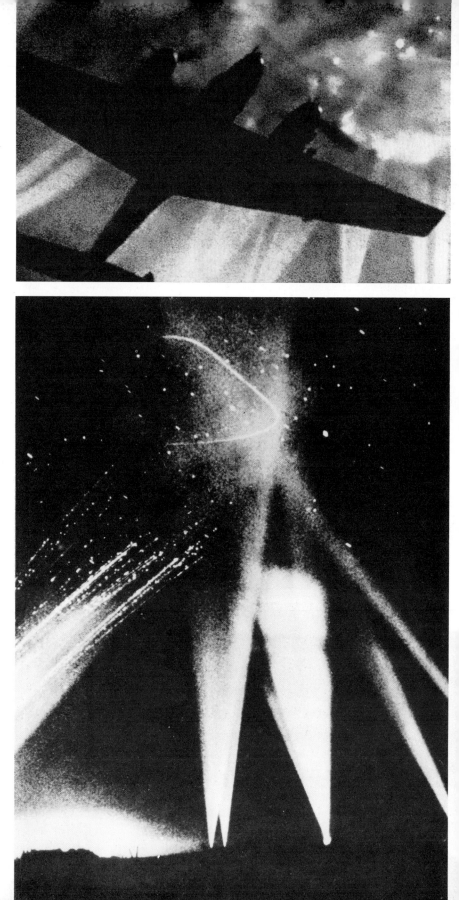

Top: A Bf 110 climbs into a sky lit-up by flak bursts and searchlights, to keep an appointment with a designated opponent.
Below: An enemy bomber is hit. The burning point in the sky appears as a bright streak on the long-exposure photograph.

36

Top: Nocturnal combat viewed from a fighter. The bomber is on the fighter's starboard beam, and the mid-upper gunner has opened fire on the Bf 110.
Below: The nightfighter turns in on the British bomber and opens fire.
Right: The burning bomber falls to earth, its flames illuminating the unbroken cloud cover.

Opposite page: Bf 110s of a Beleuchtergruppe, whose job it was to drop parachute flares into the combat area in the hope of illuminating targets for the fighters.
This page, top and middle: The burnt-out remains of an Avro Lancaster are expertly examined.
Below: The kangaroo raid symbols on this aircraft indicate an Australian crew. The last raid was on Mannheim; the name of the town has been written in, but the symbol was never to be painted.

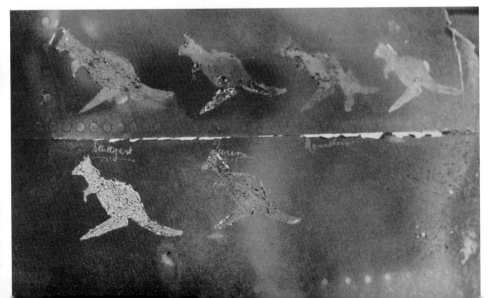

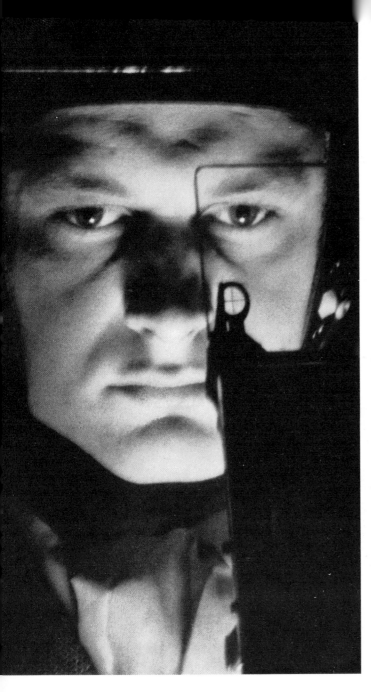
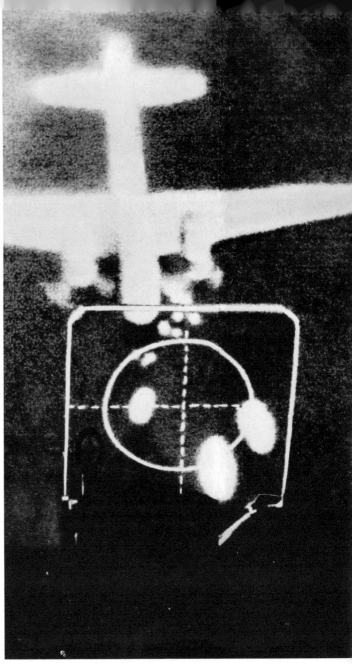

As the nightfighter pilot closes to firing range, he watches his opponent intently through the Revi (reflector gunsight). Shots strike home to the right wing root of the Wellington.

Top: This Spitfire of 306 (Polish) Squadron, RAF, was shot down while making a low-level attack on St. Trond airfield, which was the base of II./NJG 1, on 12 September 1941.

Middle: III./NJG 1's victory board.

Below: A Bf 110 of III./NJG 1 in the typical all-black finish of the early nightfighters.

41

Above: St. Trond airfield.
Left: Leutnant Greiner lights his pipe over a game of chess. On the walls of the officers' mess at St. Trond are a control yoke and various other pieces of British bomber equipment, and a victory table.
Below: St. Trond – the nightfighter station in daylight. Mechanics carry out necessary maintenance on the aircraft.

Top: A Staffel of II./NJG 1 take off, probably on a ferry flight.
Middle: Bf 110s of 8./NJG 1.
Below: Oberleutnant Helmer, then inexperienced in nightfighting.

Left: Leutnant Autenrieth hangs up a new trophy – a fuselage roundel from a British bomber – in the officers' mess at St. Trond.

Above: Major Falck on his way to a Geschwader commanders' conference; to his left is Hauptmann Steinhoff, who went on to win the Knight's Cross with Swords (Ritterkreuz mit Schwerten), and to command the first jet fighter Geschwader.

Below: During the day the machines are parked under guard on the apron. The complete absence of camouflage indicates that this photograph was taken in the early days of nightfighting.

Top: I./NJG 4 was formed out of I./ZG 26 in the spring of 1941. This aircraft is en route to Metz, the new unit's base.

Middle: Oberleutnant Becker converses with Oberfeldwebel Ruppel, at right of picture; at left is Feldwebel Poppelmeier.

Below: A Spitfire that was hit while attacking St. Trond airfield and forced to land there. (Translator's note: The aircraft appears to have been extensively repainted with spurious RAF markings, having presumably carried German colours for a time.)

45

Left: Oberleutnant Reinhold Eckardt of II./NJG 1 in conversation with an Oberleutnant of the Technical Branch, at St. Trond in the late summer of 1941. Eckardt had just recently been awarded the Ritterkreuz after his twelfth victory.
Above: Armourers adjusting the guns on Oberleutnant Eckardt's Bf 110.
Below: With the aircraft jacked-up in a horizontal position, the guns are adjusted on the firing range. A close grouping of hits on a target disc at the right distance indicates that the weapons are properly harmonized.

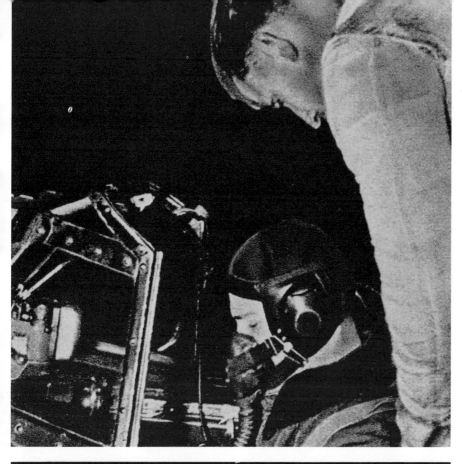

Top: A pilot is helped with his cockpit check by his ground crew chief. Here he appears to be testing his oxygen supply.
Middle: Clear for take-off. The heavy fighter roars off down the runway.
Bottom: Soon a twisting trail of fire in the sky announces another nightfighter victory.

47

Opposite page, left: On 31 May 1942 Leutnant Niklas shot down a British bomber, but in the process his Bf 110 was badly shot-up by the bomber's rear gunner, forcing him to crash-land. (Niklas was subsequently killed while attacking an American B-17 in daylight.)

Opposite page, right and below: The damage sustained by Niklas' fighter, with hits to the cockpit, nose, wing-root, port engine and fuselage.

Above: Oberfeldwebel Gildner (right) and Leutnant Hahn (left) salute the guard of honour after receiving their Ritterkreuze from General Kammhuber (centre).

Right: Oberstleutnant Falck congratulates Oberfeldwebel Gildner on his Ritterkreuz.

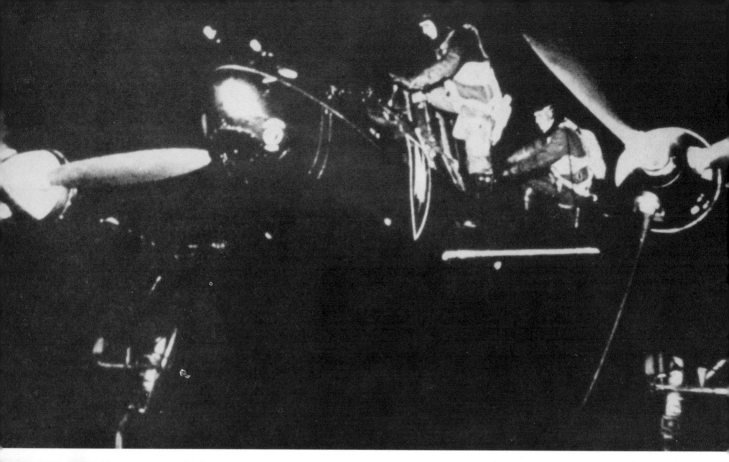

Above: Oberfeldwebel Gildner's crew boarding their machine for another operation.
Left: Gildner and Unteroffizier Müller inspect a Wellington they had shot down the previous night, 13 March 1941. The 'Wimpy' crashed at Jipsinghuizen in northern Holland.

Above: A rear gunner checks his MG 81 Z. There were times when the lives of the whole crew depended on his vigilance and the correct functioning of his weapon.
Right: The 'face' of a Bf 110 nightfighter.
Below: A pilot seen through the armoured windscreen and reflector gunsight of his Bf 110. He is wearing his oxygen mask, which, unlike its British and American equivalents, contained no microphone; instead, a throat microphone was standard in the Luftwaffe.

Left: Oberleutnant Lent received his Ritterkreuz on 30 August 1941, after eight day and fourteen night victories.
Right: The fin of Lent's Bf 110 with thirty victories chalked up.
Below: Lent establishes II./NJG 1, based at St. Trond, in November 1941.

52

Top: Helmut Lent, now a Hauptmann, listens on the radio telephone to his crews in action.
Middle: After the real action, it's paperwork time. Hauptmann Herget is seen here writing-up his report.
Below: The first nightfighter version of the Ju 88 is delivered to the front line; here, one appears in formation with a Bf 110.

Left: Details of crews in action; time of take-off and allotted sector are noted on a blackboard in the operations room.
Below: Major Herget and his crew prepare for their next sortie.
Opposite page, top: A Kette (three-plane formation) of 7./NJG 4's 110s sets out on a ferry flight.
Opposite page, below: 3C + AR, a Bf 110 F-2, was flown by Oberleutnant Kamp, Staffelkapitän of 7./NJG 4.

Right: One of hundreds of night combats, as visualized by an artist. The bomber is a Halifax.
Below: The Avro Lancaster was probably the most redoubtable opponent among British bombers. (This one was from 1661 Heavy Conversion Unit, and therefore a trainer.)

Oberleutnant Lent whiles away the time to his next sortie with an expert game of skat.

The telephone rings, and the nerve-racking wait is over. Lent receives the order to 'scramble'.

Armourers work around the clock to keep the guns in perfect working order.

Top: In Britain, the first bombers, such as this Short Stirling of 218 Squadron, taxi out to take off.

Middle: Major Falck, Kommodore of NJG 1, prepares to meet them. Below the cockpit of his aircraft is the ladybird emblem of his former Staffel, 2./ZG 76, with which he was very successful.

Below: In the last rays of the setting sun a Bf 110 sits fuelled and armed ready to fly against the night-time foe.

59

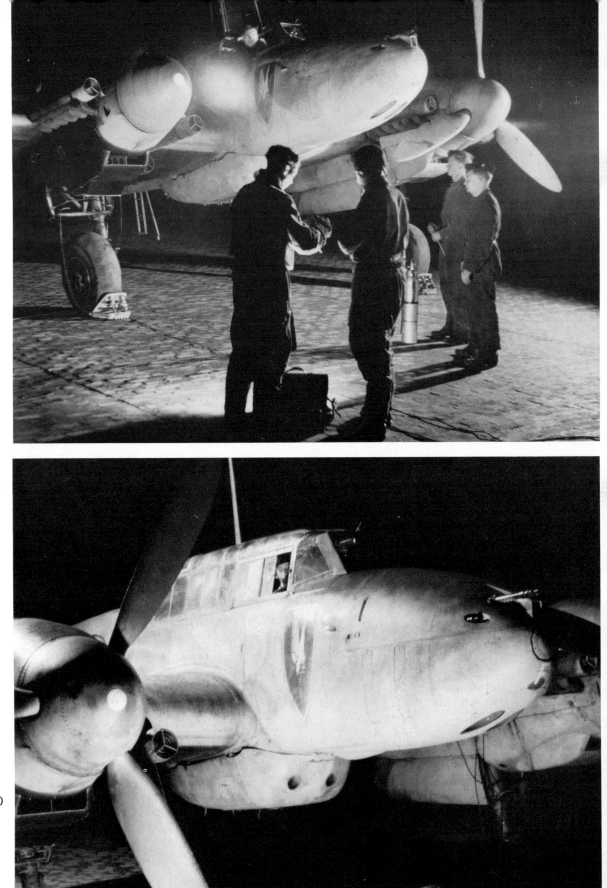

Top: Mechanics work by floodlight on a defective engine. Thanks to these men, the nightfighter arm enjoyed a high level of aircraft serviceability.
Below: The under-fuselage weapons pack was not often fitted to Bf 110 nightfighters.

60

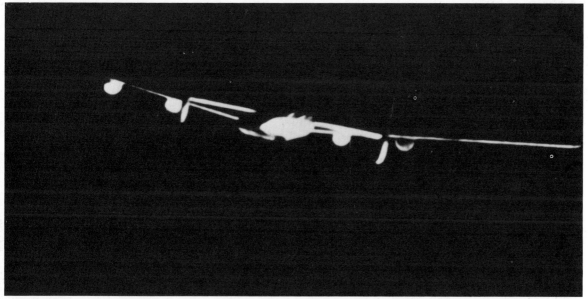

Top: Searchlights cast probing fingers skywards in search of the enemy.
Middle: A training model shows how a Lancaster looks when illuminated from below by searchlights.
Below: A Bf 110 closes in on the bomber from the left, its wing tanks reflecting the light. This is a fair simulation of the appearance of a night combat.

Above: The night-fighters' losses rose along with their successes. This is the funeral of a crew which included Oberfeldwebel Scherflin and Unteroffizier Besa of IV./NJG 1 at Leuwarden.

Right: Hauptmann Jabs, Kommandeur of the 4th Gruppe, takes leave of his fallen comrades.

62

Top: A last, expert once-over by the crew chief. All ready to go. **Below:** Scramble! Aircrews go to their machines along an avenue of British propeller blades, while RAF roundels decorate the walls of the crew room.

63

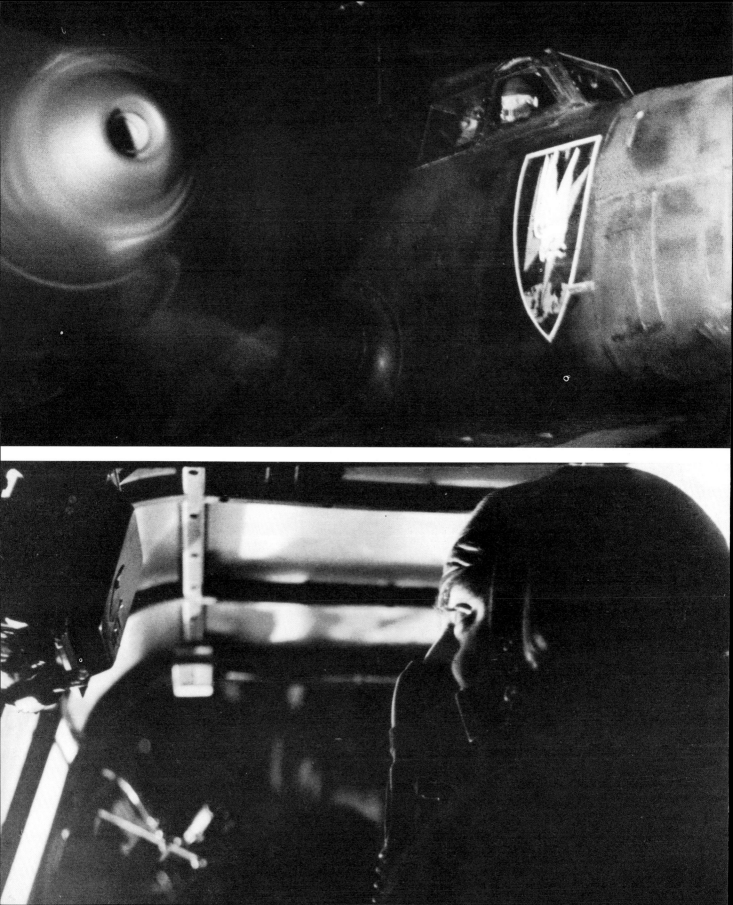

Opposite page: A Bf 110, engines at full revs, awaits the signal to take off. The radio operator (below) checks his instruments.
Top: This Bf 110, flown by Leutnant Mathes of II./NJG 1, burst a tyre and overturned on landing at Deelen on 18 February, 1941.
Middle: A highly apposite aphorism on the workshop wall at NJG 1's base; it translates approximately as "The Lord 'elps them as 'elps themselves".
Below: Yet another chance for the 'black men' to demonstrate their expertise at getting a 'beat-up mill' back in service in next to no time.

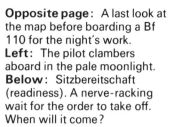

Opposite page: A last look at the map before boarding a Bf 110 for the night's work.
Left: The pilot clambers aboard in the pale moonlight.
Below: Sitzbereitschaft (readiness). A nerve-racking wait for the order to take off. When will it come?

Left: Oberleutnant Becker receives the Ritterkreuz from General Kammhuber on 1 July 1942, having shot down twenty-five aircraft. As well as being an expert pilot, Becker introduced many new ideas and improvements into nightfighting.
Right: Oberleutnante Lent, Becker and Gildner salute their Kommandeur.
Below: To end Oberleutnant Becker's investiture ceremony, General Kammhuber reviews the parade with his successful officers.

Above and below: This slightly damaged Stirling was forced down and later flown to Gilze Rijen for testing.
Right: Leutnant König of III./NJG 3 practises cockpit readiness with his mascot. In 1942 König lost an eye in combat, and was removed from night duties. 'King', as his colleagues called him, transferred to day fighting and, as Staffelkapitän of 3./JG 11 and later as Kommandeur of I./JG 11, became one of the most successful 'defenders of the Reich'. He was killed in action on 24 May 1944 near Kaltenkirchen.

Top: II./NJG 1 at St. Trond receive a visit from General Christiansen. Major Lent, Kommandeur of the Gruppe, accompanies the distinguished guest on his way to inspect the guard of honour.
Middle: General Christiansen greets Hauptmann Jabs, Staffelkapitän of 11./NJG 1.
Below: The General takes his leave of the 2nd Gruppe.

70

Combined Nightfighting

Combined nightfighting was introduced between the middle and end of 1941. The new system arose from the need to use the available ground (flak) and air defences as efficiently as possible. Combined nightfighting forces were envisaged as being concentrated around Kiel, Hamburg, Bremen, Duisburg, Cologne, Frankfurt, Darmstadt/Mannheim and Munich and, in fact, the system was only used in those areas. The detailed composition of Kombinierte Nachtjagd was as follows: the district to be defended was divided into three sectors, each of which had a radar station equipped with a long-range Freya (named after a goddess who owned a magic necklace which was kept for her by a deity who could see for 100 miles) and two Würzburg-Riese (Giant Würzburg) installations. The procedure began in the same way as had Helle Nachtjagd; raiders detected by the Freya were tracked over the fighter area by one Würzburg while the other directed a fighter to intercept them. Information from the two Würzburg teams was passed on to anti-aircraft divisional headquarters, where it was evaluated and converted into positions on a table map; this was made of frosted glass and the aircraft locations were projected onto it from below as blue and red spots. Thus the 'Seeburg Table' showed the tactical situation from minute to minute, and the Flakleitoffizier informed the searchlight and flak batteries accordingly, while the Jägerleitoffizier guided the fighter to its target. Flak was normally limited to below the fighters' operating height of 4,000 metres, but the Divisionskommandeur could authorize them to fire above that altitude if the fighter was unlikely to be hit.

However, for various reasons this system did not always work as its inventor had intended. Often the flak division commander, whether from personal ambition or through poorly interpreted data, failed to cease fire at the correct time, or else a fighter on a bomber's tail would not break off before it flew into the flak zone. Thus, it was not rare for fighters to be shot down by their own flak. These losses ultimately led to the abandonment of Kombinierte Nachtjagd as a failure.

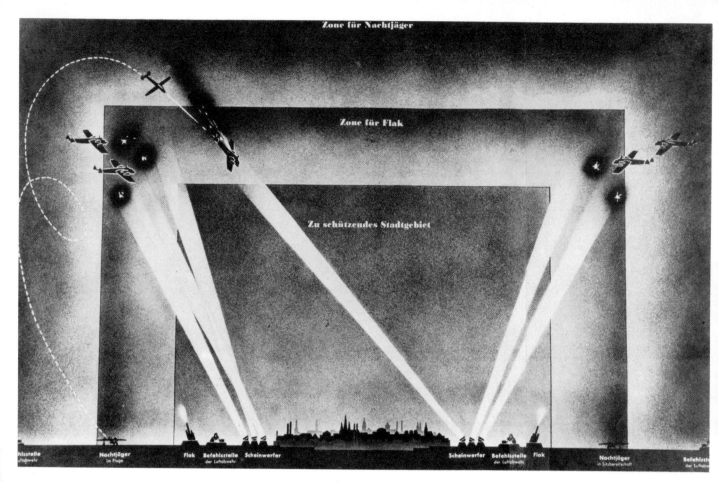

Above: This artist's impression clearly demonstrates the principle of combined nightfighting. Why this remained in the realm of theory is explained in the introduction to this chapter.

Left: A Giant Würzburg. The nightfighters' ground organization has entered the electronic age too.

Below: The information coming from the Würzburg radars is collated on the Seeburg Table, named after its inventor. The positions of both friendly and enemy aircraft are indicated by blue and red light spots projected on the glass table-top from below.

Preparing for work: a Bf 110 of NJG 3.

Above: A Bf 110 of II./NJG 1's Stabsschwarm (Staff Flight), coded G9 + DB, taxis out to the runway.
Left: Clusters of flares, known with grim humour to both sides as 'Christmas trees', often led the fighters to their quarry. The flares were dropped over the target by the British Pathfinders to mark the aiming point for the following bombers.
Below: Scramble! The crews pile into their machines.

Top: At the same time, the flak prepares for action. Sound locators supply additional information on the position of the bomber formation.
Below: The gun-layer feeds the latest coordinates into the 8.8cm gun's predictor.

76

Fire!

Left and above: The light flak has also opened fire; a combination of tracer ammunition and 'camera shake' traces weird shapes in the night sky.
Below: A salvo from a battery of 8.8cm flak. Searchlight beams, phosphorus fires, tracer trails, gun smoke and the flaming bursts of 8.8cm shells all combine to form a spectral backdrop to this nightly drama.

Top: The wreckage of British bombers bears witness to the severity of the previous night's battle.
Middle: The body of an American crewman; he baled-out too low, and his parachute failed to open in time.
Below: Some of the inhabitants of Oberbieber viewing the undercarriage of a recently-crashed bomber which has flattened much of the neighbourhood.

Top: A 2cm Vierlingsflak (four-barrelled AA gun) in action.
Middle: This radar set, specially developed for directing flak, has evidently enjoyed some success.
Below: 3.7cm flak shoots down a low-flying bomber.
Opposite page: As has already been intimated, combined nightfighting had serious disadvantages; many fighters were shot down by friendly flak. G9 + BC, flown by Leutnant Uellenbeck, force-landed at Schleswig at 2.23am on 9 May 1941.

Right and below: The seat-type parachute was put on over the life-jacket just before boarding the aircraft – an uncomfortable perch for what was often a long period of readiness.

Opposite page, top: Scramble at II./NJG 1. Two of the crew are already aboard, and the gunner is just climbing the ladder.

Opposite page, below: 3C + LR and 3C + GR, both of 7./NJG 4, fly to take position in their allotted sectors.

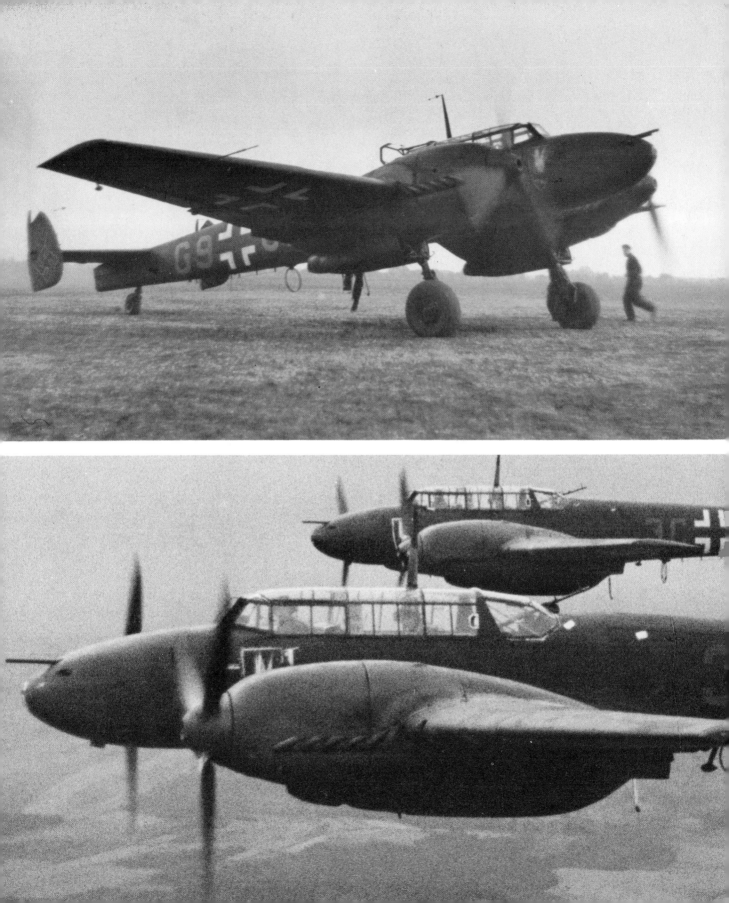

Above: A group of airmen at Stade; first row, left to right: Sosna, König, Borchers, Nacke, Jabs, Lettnig, Medical Officer (unidentified), Hüttenrauch, Wagner and Kark; second row, left to right: Löffelmann, Glaiber, Fietmann, Hahn, Radecke, Sangwald and Drewes.
Opposite page: Many filled the nerve-racking wait between actions with a game of chess.

Top: Helmut Lent briefs his crews before take-off.
Middle and below: One after another the fighters taxi out. The runway was briefly illuminated just before take-off.
Opposite page: A German city on fire. At the beginning of the British air offensive against German cities, the targets were limited to military installations and armament production centres. The German nightfighters, although few in number and not always used to full advantage, put up a heroic fight, but could not prevent the devastation that such attacks achieved.

86

Top: Major Streib arrives at Venlo to take over NJG 1, 1 July 1942. The outgoing Kommodore, another founder-member of the nightfighter service, is Wolfgang Falck, here seen cordially greeting his successor.
Middle: Oberstleutnant Falck, who has been summoned to take up a staff post, delivers a parting speech to his Geschwader.
Below: Werner Streib formally takes command.

88

Long-range Nightfighting

A further Gruppe was established, simultaneously with I./NJG 1. It was designated from the beginning as a long-range fighter Gruppe and accordingly equipped with Do 17s and Ju 88s. This nightfighter unit was led by Hauptmann Heyse, and was later, as I./NJG 2, to become the nucleus of a highly successful Geschwader. The aim of long-range nightfighting was to attack the enemy where he least expected it, namely over his own bases in Britain. One tactic of the Fernnachtjägd was to join the returning British formations and attack them during their landing approach, when they were at their most vulnerable. Another stratagem was to listen with powerful receivers to the radio traffic in Britain, on the premise that plane-to-plane conversations increased considerably as sets were tuned in at the beginning of a raid. As soon as a rise in radio activity was reported, fighters already loitering in British airspace were directed to the supposed British assembly point. The British bombers, engrossed in the complex manoeuvres of forming up, were then an easy target for the intruders.

Specialists arose among the pilots, who developed new variations on the standard tactics, and Fernnachtjagd, successful from the beginning, became even more effective. It was thus all the more surprising and incomprehensible when on 12 October 1941 Hitler ordered the abandonment of long-range nightfighting. Several reasons were given for this decision. One was the fact that Fernnachtjagd victory claims could not be checked, and another was the need to parade shot-down enemy aircraft before the civilian population, who were having to spend more and more nights in cellars and shelters. Despite the ban, many crews continued to fly sorties over Britain, and scored victories. Long-range nightfighting was officially reinstated at the beginning of 1945, but owing to the general state of affairs only a few token victories resulted.

A Do 17 Kauz of II./NJG 2 in its dispersal pen.

Top: This Ju 88C-6 belongs to the Ergänzungsgruppe (Reserve Gruppe) of NJG 2.

Middle: The Ju 88C-6s of E/NJG 2 were stationed at Gilze Rijen, Holland in May 1943. This machine was flown by Leutnant Bruno Heinrich, Unteroffizier Heinrich Scholl and Gefreiter Karl Chuss.

Below: A Ju 88C-6 shot down on the landing approach by British night intruders on 9 January 1943.

Top: A particularly successful long-range nightfighter crew was that of Heinz Rökker, here seen strapping in. Rökker was awarded Oak Leaves to his Knight's Cross.
Middle: Rökker and his crew, 2./NJG 2; from left to right, Carlos Nugent (search radar operator), Heinz Rökker (pilot), Franz Franz (ground crew chief), Hans-Heinz Matter (radio operator), Friedrich Wefelmeier (observer). This photograph was taken in spring 1945, by which time long-range nightfighting had been officially reinstated.
Below: The traditional egg flip is drunk after a successful sortie over Britain. The location is Twente, Holland in the spring of 1945.

92

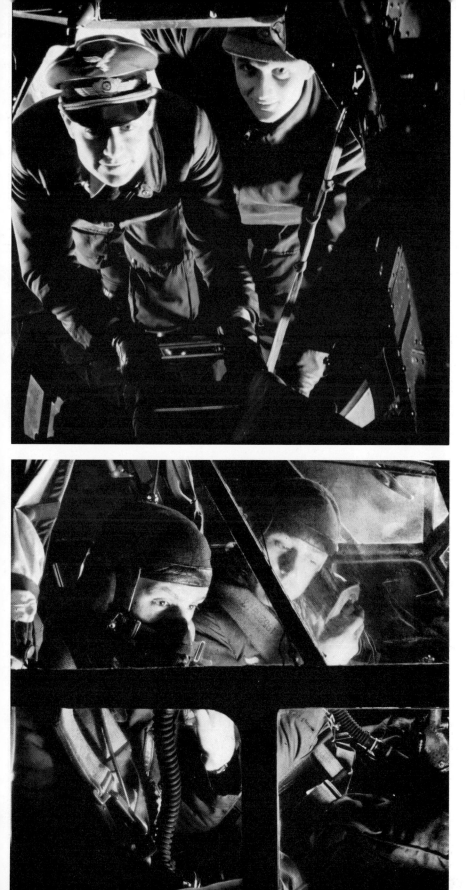

Left: A crew boarding their Ju 88 for the nightly raid on the British Isles.
Below: Oxygen on.

Top: A radio operator's 'office'; at right, an SN 2 radar set.
Below left: The rear gunner. His job of protecting the aircraft was particularly difficult in the dark.
Below right: Chocks are pulled away from the Ju 88's wheels.

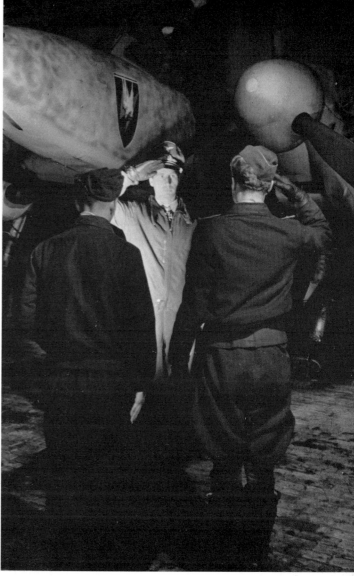

The end of a successful flight for Oberleutnant Strüning, who received Oak Leaves to his Ritterkreuz on 20 July 1944.

Oberleutnant Paul Semrau reports back from a sortie in which he scored two victories. On 1 November 1944 Semrau was appointed Kommodore of NJG 2.

Top: Each Geschwader had an Ergänzungs-gruppe or reserve unit, in which new crews were eased into operational conditions by their more experienced colleagues.
Middle: A Ju 88 plays target for a crew in training. Of the various attack patterns practised, the commonest was to approach the enemy from behind and below.
Below: A flight of Ju 88s approaches its airfield near Gilze Rijen at dusk.

96

Top and middle: This Ju 88C-6 received several hits over Britain and crash-landed short of its home airfield. Mechanics from the airfield maintenance unit attempt to raise the belly-landed aircraft with air bags (middle) so that it can be carried back to base.
Below: The Ju 88C-4 was a conversion of the Ju 88A-4 bomber. Surprisingly, the unnecessary and drag-producing dive brakes were not removed.

97

Generalmajor Kammhuber and Leutnant Hahn just after a Knight's Cross investiture. Hahn was the most successful night intruder pilot until his death on 11 October 1941, when he collided with a British aircraft over England.

Russia, Africa and Special Missions

The success rate of nightfighters in the eastern and southern theatres did not compare with that of the home defenders, since few night units were sent to these parts, and they lacked any specialized control organization. Added to these problems were inadequately equipped aircraft (many without any form of radar) and the huge expanses of land to be covered.

In the East

For a long time in this theatre there were only a few attempts at nightfighting, undertaken on personal initiative. Leutnant Leykauf of JG 54 shot down six Soviet bombers while flying a Bf 109G on the night of 23 June 1941. Other pilots flew their regular unit machines; for example, Unteroffizier Döring of KG 55 flew an He 111 bomber fitted with several forward-firing guns in the nose. Even Fw 58 communications and Fw 189 Army-cooperation aircraft were pressed into service against the very low and slow-flying Russian ground-attack units. Makeshift nightfighter formations arose piecemeal, and these were eventually designated and equipped as proper nightfighter units. As they were joined and instructed by experienced crews from the home front, the situation changed for the better, but it was not until the establishment of IV./NJG 5 under Prinz zu Sayn-Wittgenstein that the nightfighter arm in the East began to score regularly.

Africa

The main nightfighter unit in Africa was I./NJG 2, but the rest of the Geschwader was occasionally sent to join them. Besides their intended rôle, NJG 2's Ju 88s also had to fly escort for convoys and air transports. As the situation changed, and it was usually for the worse, the Luftwaffe units had to move their bases. After the surrender of the Afrika Korps, the nightfighters operated from Sicily. When the Allies landed at Palermo, the remaining nightfighters moved to central Italy.

Special missions

On 12 February 1942 the nightfighters of NJG 1 took part in operation 'Donnerkeil' (Thunderbolt). This was the break-out of the battlecruisers *Scharnhorst* and *Gneisenau* and the heavy cruiser, *Prinz Eugen* from Brest and their eastward dash up the Channel to Wilhelmshaven and Kiel. Bf 110s of NJG 1 took over the convoy's air cover at dusk.

Above: Oberstleutnant Falck's Bf 110 on an airfield near Bucharest, autumn 1943.
Left: Falck established the Eastern Command of the Inspectorate of Nightfighters (Inspekteur der Nachtjäger) in Rumania. The defence of the Ploesti oilfields was to be organized from this command post. Falck was awarded a high Rumanian decoration for fulfilling this task.

Top: Oberstleutnant Falck in conversation with a Rumanian general.
Middle: Departure time approaches. Alongside his aircraft Falck says goodbye to one of his colleagues.
Below: Falck boards his machine for the flight home.

A heavily-armed Bf 110F-4 of NJG 100, which operated mainly in the East, approaches to land.

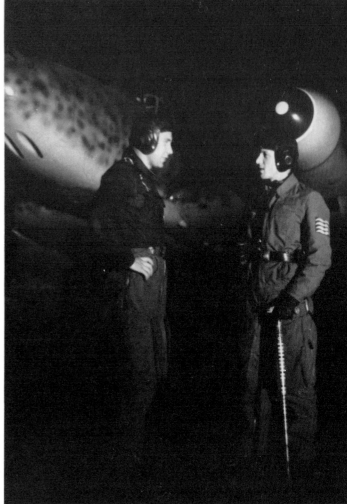

Hauptmann Prinz zu Sayn-Wittgenstein was particularly successful in Russia. The fin of his Ju 88 here shows five Eastern Front victories, and many more were to come.

10./(NJ)ZG 1 had an equally successful night ace. Oberfeldwebel Josef Kociok, seen here in the Crimea in the spring of 1943, amassed thirty-three victories in the East, of which twenty-one were obtained at night.

Left: Oberleutnant Josef Pützkuhl, one of the many other unsung pilots, radio operators and gunners who did their duty in the East. Although their names are not so well known, these pilots were no less keen or devoted, and continued to fly against ever stronger opposition.
Above: NJG 100 was deployed mainly in the East. One of its Bf 110s is here seen being serviced.
Below: A Schwarm of Bf 110s from NJG 100 sets out on a day sortie. The Ju 52 in the foreground may be identified as a member of the same unit by the badge to the left of the cockpit.

Far left, top: Leutnant Spoden reports to Oberleutnant Johnen after a successful outing.
Far left, below: This train carried equipment, supplies, spares and ground crew from base to ever-changing base.
Left, top: Leutnant Gustav Francsi confers with his radio operator before taking off.
Left, below: Francsi was the most successful nightfighter pilot on the Eastern Front. On 29 October 1944, after twenty-nine victories in that theatre, he received the Ritterkreuz from the Jagdführer Ostpreussen (Fighter Commander-in-Chief East Prussia), Oberstleutnant Nordmann, at left of picture.

Nightfighters also operated in the Mediterranean theatre. Most were from NJG 2, but when necessary units from other Geschwader were drafted in.
Right: L1+ was the code of 1./NJG 3, here photographed on an airfield in Sicily.
Below: A Bf 110 of 1./NJG 3 sets out on a maritime patrol.

Top: A ferry flight from Sicily to Crete.
Middle: Besides nightfighting, 1./NJG 3's duties included convoy escort, as here.
Below: Feldwebel Hütscher with his radio operator. In the background is their Bf 110 of 1./NJG 3, Argos 1941.

Top: As this Ju 88 of NJG 2 rolls to a stop, the ventral gondola is already open to admit some welcome fresh air. This hatch also formed the crew door.

Middle: The Ju 88 is off again after a brief refuelling stop. 1./NJG 2 was also engaged in convoy escort duties.

Below: R4+CH of 1./NJG 2 lost her under-carriage on landing, as a result of combat damage to a hydraulic line.

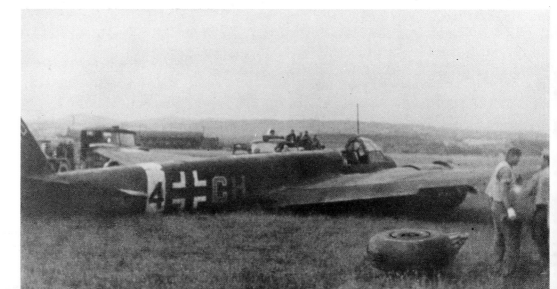

Top: In 1942 Leutnant Rökker of 2./NJG 2 crash-landed in this Ju 88A-4, Work No. 5664 at Catania in Sicily. The dinghy is being removed from its stowage in the top of the rear fuselage.
Below: Members of Rökker's crew; on the left is Georg Frieben (observer) and on the right the crew chief. Rökker's Ju 88 R4+FR was stationed at Castelretrano in Sicily on 9 June 1943.

Top: VC EK was flown by Hauptmann Eistermann of 6./NJG 3.
Middle: Oberstleutnant Falck's Bf 110 goes up in flames during a British raid on Iráklion in Crete in September 1942.
Below: Spring in Sicily. An almost romantic picture, but the war is ever-present. Even III./ZG 26's Zerstörer were called upon to operate as night-fighters over Southern Italy.

On 12 February 1942 the joint Kriegsmarine and Luftwaffe Operation 'Donnerkeil' (Thunderbolt) was mounted. This was the code-name for the break-out through the English Channel of the battle-cruisers *Scharnhorst* and *Gneisenau* and the heavy cruiser *Prinz Eugen*. The nightfighters took over responsibility for the flotilla's air cover at dusk.

Top: Several Bf 110s of NJG 1 over the Norwegian fjords at the end of Operation 'Donnerkeil'.
Middle: *Scharnhorst* at full speed. In the evening the night-fighters of NJG 1 relieved ZG 76's Bf 110 day fighters and accompanied the convoy for the rest of its journey.
Below: A Schwarm of Bf 110s overtakes a German minesweeper.

Right: A nightfighter circles above the Naval Squadron as it heads for Kiel.
Below: A Rotte (pair) of Bf 110s skim past the Kriegsmarine ships.

The Himmelbett System: The Beginning of Dark Nightfighting

Summer 1941 saw the introduction of a new system, code-named 'Himmelbett' (four-poster bed), the principles of which would remain in use for the rest of the war. A whole network of Himmelbett zones was set up next to the searchlight belt from the middle of 1941. The circular, controlled zones were laid out both side by side and in depth, the radius of each circle being the range of the radar equipment. Würzburg had a range of 35km (21 miles), and Würzburg-Riese (Giant Würzburg), which had a 7.50m (24½ft) dish and entered service in 1942, could track aircraft up to 60–70km (36–42 miles) away. A Himmelbett station was equipped with the following: 1, a Freya radar to acquire targets for the more precise Würzburg sets; 2, a Giant Würzburg to track the bomber; 3, a Giant Würzburg to direct the fighter; and 4, a translucent Seeburg Table, on which friendly and enemy aircraft were represented by coloured spots of light.

Using the various technical means mentioned above, the Himmelbett system worked as follows. The search Freya detected the enemy at about 150km range (90 miles) and passed the target formation to a Red Würzburg unit. Red designated the radar which tracked the bomber, while blue stood for the set which guided the fighter to it. This fighter, already at operational altitude, had to orbit a radio beacon in the controlled airspace during the preliminary location phase. A second fighter remained crewed and ready to take off, and a third aircraft and its crew was held in reserve. The fighter control officers, reading the relative positions from the Seeburg Table, then vectored the fighter onto its quarry.

The critical disadvantage of the system was that at any given time only one fighter was airborne in any control zone. The British soon realized this, and concentrated their bomber stream into one zone, so that only a maximum of three fighters could be brought to bear. When this drawback was recognized by Luftwaffe leaders, the Himmelbett system was modified.

Left: A Himmelbett installation: the intruders are detected by the Freya radar (at right of picture) at long range. A Würzburg-Riese (left) then takes over to supply more exact measurements of altitude, formation size, speed and direction. A second Würzburg follows the nightfighter and vectors it to the enemy.

Below: Generalmajor Kammhuber's nightfighter organization: the circles at left are the Himmelbett controlled zones, each given an animal code-name. The squares with Roman numerals are searchlight zones, the province of Helle Nachtjagd. Combined nightfighting was concentrated around industrial centres, such as Berlin, Cologne and the Ruhr Valley.

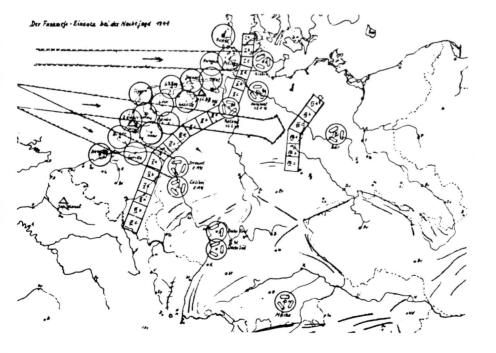

Der Funkmeß-Einsatz bei der Nachtjagd 1941

Wie werden unsere Nachtjäger an den angreifenden feindlichen Verband herangeführt? Diese Frage interessiert den Laien ganz besonders, wenn er im Wehrmachtbericht die hohen nächtlichen Abschußziffern liest. Daß es hier nicht ganz mit „natürlichen" Dingen zugeht, ist ihm klar, da ja der Nachtjäger den Feind nicht sieht, wenn dieser unter Ausnutzung völliger Dunkelheit oder unsichtigen Wetters anfliegt. Es ist ihm klar, daß hier hochentwickelte Geräte gewissermaßen als „Auge" benutzt werden, und zwar von der Erde aus, die die Nachtjäger an den Feind „heranführen", bis sie ihn entweder an seinen Umrissen oder an den Auspuffflammen der Motore erkennen können. Die technischen Einzelheiten entziehen sich naturgemäß der näheren Beschreibung, und auch unsere Zeichnung oben entspricht nicht der Wirklichkeit. Die Zeichnung rechts zeigt: Feindberührung! Der Nachtjäger hat unter sich die vierreihigen Auspuffflämmchen erkannt. Fast senkrecht stürzend wirft er sich in den feindlichen Pulk, visiert eine Viermotorige an, drückt auf alle Knöpfe, und knapp am Leitwerk des Bombers vorbeisausend, sieht er auch schon die ersten Stichflammen aus Motor und Rumpf des Gegners lodern. Noch während er seine Me aus diesem Sturz abfängt, sucht er nach einem neuen Opfer. Einem unserer erfolgreichen Nachtjäger, dem Major Herget, von dem unten erzählt wird, gelang es, innerhalb von 50 Minuten acht Gegner zu erledigen.

Zeichnungen: NSKK-Kriegsberichter Theo Matejko

In der 50. Minute:
Der 8te Abschuss!
Major Hergett, der Meister der Doubletten

Von Kriegsberichter WOLFGANG KÜCHLER

Es soll heute hier versucht werden, das Bild eines der nächtlichen Kämpfer in Deutschlands Himmel zu zeichnen. Die Geschichte des Nachtjägers Major Herget, der kürzlich innerhalb von fünfzig Minuten acht viermotorige Bomber bei einem einzigen Einsatz abschoß und der mit 46 Nacht- und 14 Tagesabschüssen zu unseren besten und erfolgreichsten Fliegern zählt, ist kennzeichnend für den Geist, der die deutschen Nachtjäger beseelt.

Opposite page, top left: Once the information on the incoming British raid has been analysed, orders are issued to the nightfighter units.

Opposite page, top right: Worried faces at Luftflotte Reich (Home Air Fleet) headquarters. The aerial situation is becoming ever more threatening.

Opposite page, below: Hectic activity in the Luftflotte Reich operations room at Berlin-Wannsee, summer 1944; left to right, Generalmajor Nielsen, Chief of Staff, Oberst Falck, and Oberleutnant Wever, son of the Luftwaffe's first General Chief of Staff.

Above: An article from *Der Adler*, describing a particularly successful night's work by Wilhelm Herget, one of many former Zerstörer pilots in the nightfighter service. The headline runs: "In the 50th minute: the 8th victory!".

Above and left: Hauptmann Prinz zu Sayn-Wittgenstein views the wreck of a British bomber which he had shot down the previous night.
Below: On 2 October 1942 Oberleutnant Prinz zu Sayn-Wittgenstein, with twenty-two 'kills', receives the Ritterkreuz from General Kammhuber.

Top: Dornier contributed to the nightfighter effort with a converted bomber, the Do 217N, which was of little use as it lacked speed and manoeuvrability; it was slower both in level flight and in a dive than the British Lancaster and Halifax.
Middle: A crash-landed Do 217. Undercarriage failures were a major cause of take-off and landing accidents.
Below: A Do 217N. Even the heavy armament failed to offset the above disadvantages. Only as a long-range night intruder did the Do 217 stand any chance of success.

Top: Göring arrives to inspect NJG 1 in autumn 1943.
Left: Hermann Göring delivers one of his pithy speeches; to his right is Oberstleutnant Streib, Kommodore of NJG 1.
Below right: The Luftwaffe chief talks to Hauptmann Meurer, Kommandeur of I./NJG 1; at centre is Generalmajor Kammhuber and, behind Göring, Generaloberst Loerzer.
Right top: Above the Reichsmarschall's epaulette we recognize Jabs, Kommandeur of IV./NJG 1, and, to his right, Schnaufer, Drewes, Vinke and Pfeiffer.
Bottom: The 'Fat Man' congratulates Vinke on his Ritterkreuz; left to right, Loerzer, unknown, Göring, Rolland, Pottharst, Fengler, Rühle, Scherfling, Vinke and Pfeiffer.

Hermann Göring's speech appears to be going on and on.

Göring, hands buried carelessly in pockets, receives Hauptmann Jabs's report.

124

Top: With four MG 17s and four MG 151s the Do 217N could deliver a heavy concentration of fire.

Middle: The Dornier's upward-firing armament of four cannons is clearly visible on the top of the rear fuselage in this picture.

Below: The pilot's position in a Do 217N.

125

Above: Gefechtsstand (command post) 'Sokrates' near Stade; the nightfighters were directed by the divisional commanders from such control centres as this.

Right: Inside a divisional control room. These establishments, jokingly referred to as Kammhuber Cinemas or Gefechtssopernhäuser (Ops Opera Houses), were costly in terms of personnel and technical resources, and critics maintained that the results did not justify the expense, for no amount of machinery and organization could guarantee an interception and 'kill'. 1, Divisional Commander, a general, and his assistant, the Chief of Operations Section. Next to him are the liaison officers for flak, Air Intelligence, Army and Navy. The fighter control officers in front of him are in direct contact with the nightfighters in the air. On the basis of the latest information, they direct the fighters to the enemy. This did not always work. 2, A 14m high glass screen forms the focal point of the operations room. On it is

...isplayed the whole of the region defended by the nightfighter division. Behind the screen are projectors which show the updated ...ositions of friend and foe as blue and red spots of light. 3, From the back of the room, lines and arrows are projected onto the screen ...o show the path of the enemy bomber stream. 4, A group of officers evaluate reports as they come in. 5, A bomber stream projected on ...he screen. 6, The stream has split up, and one section is attacking a large town. 7, The airborne fighters are directed to the town under ...ttack. 8, The two square maps show the neighbouring divisions from which the enemy came and through which he is expected to ...etreat. The other two show the territory of the entire Korps, the next unit up the scale; the last map in fact covers the whole of Europe, ...nd on it the enemy aircraft are tracked from their first appearance over the mainland until they return home.

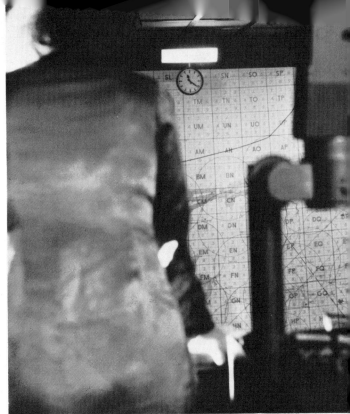

Left: Jägerleitoffiziere
(Fighter controllers)
Right: The main map.
Below: Spot projectors and
their operators.

Above: Evaluation of incoming data from the Würzburg-Riese radars.
Right: General Grabmann (left) and Major Streib, probably in the control room at Deelen.
Below: Behind the fighter controllers is a board indicating the state of readiness of the various fighter units. In the left-hand column are the airfields, then the units, then take-off and combat times.

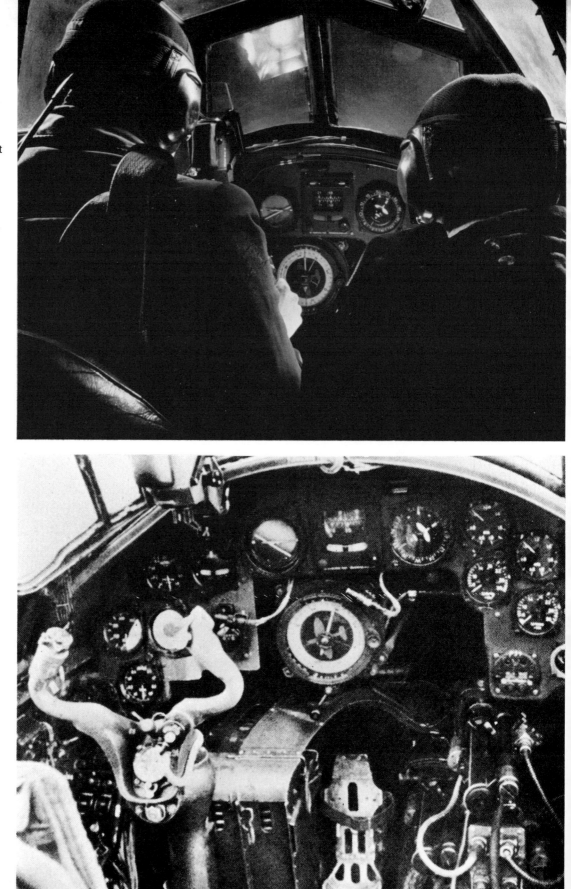

Top: The crew of a Ju 88 prepare for action.
Below: The instrument panel of a Ju 88 night-fighter. Behind the control column are the ammunition boxes for the heavy machine-guns in the starboard side of the nose.

130

Right: The Japanese Ambassador Mr. Oshima visits Stade, where he is welcomed by Major Heinz Nacke.
Above: Mr Oshima shows an especial interest in the Bf 110 aircraft.
Below: At the time of the Ambassador's visit, parts of II./ZG 76 had just converted to the nightfighter rôle. Their Bf 110s still carried the 'shark's mouth' emblem which had made them so well-known in their previous Zerstörer duties.

Above: Not even ice and snow prevented the 'black men', the mechanics, from going about their responsible business.
Below: A last handshake, and the Schwarm is ready to set off for the Himmelbett zones.

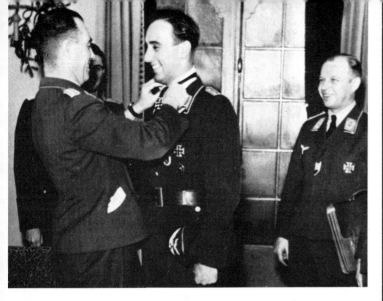

Above: Oberleutnant Wolfgang Schnaufer with forty-two victories receives the Ritterkreuz from Generalmajor Schmid on 3 January 1944.
Right: Major Günther Radusch behind the Revi of his Bf 110.
Below: Rising successes were balanced by a rise in casualties. Oberleutnant Schnaufer, Kapitän of 12./NJG 1, pronounces the last words over the graves of Leutnant Rühle's crew.

Opposite page: A Bf 110, which had crash-landed after sustaining damage in combat with a British night intruder fighter, is raised on air bags for transport back to the repair shops.

Above: As the air battle over Germany intensifies relentlessly, new nightfighter crews are trained. A formation of Bf 110s from a nightfighter school on a navigational practice flight.

Left: An airman brought down at sea depends on his dinghy for salvation, but first he must practice getting into it in the swimming pool.

Top: A new trainee crew; note that they are wearing the bomber-type full helmet rather than the net type usually favoured by fighter crews. (Translator's note: Reliable sources state that this is the difference between winter and summer headgear, but it may be that fighter crews preferred the net helmet at all times.)

Below: A captured B-17 used at Deelen for attack training, June 1943.

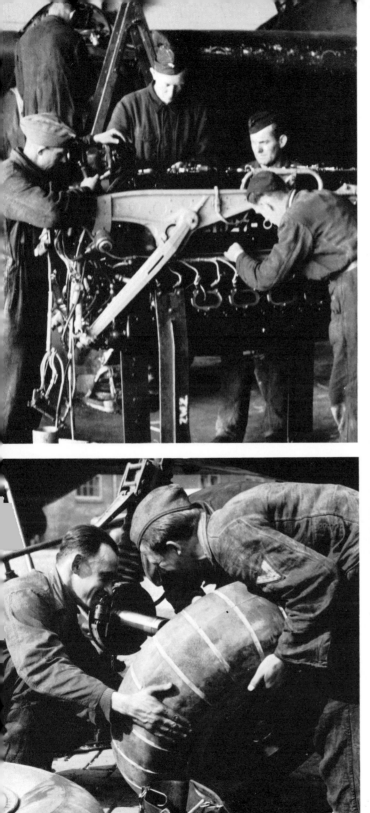

Without the tireless and selfless work of the technicians, also known as 'black men' because of their black overalls, the success rate and survival chances of the aircrew would have been greatly reduced.

Left: Walter Ehle, one of the trailblazers of night-fighting, became Kommandeur of II./NJG 1 in October 1940.
Below: 29 August, 1943; Major Ehle (thirty-one victories) and Oberfeldwebel Kollak (right) receive the Knight's Cross from General Kammhuber at St. Trond.
Right: The funeral of Major Ehle and his crew, who were all killed when the runway lights at St. Trond failed as they were landing on 17 November 1943. Oberstleutnant Werner Streib (right) is one of the many paying their last respects.

Left: In the control room Major Prinz zur Lippe-Weissenfeld describes the next mission. On the board behind him are the names of airfields and combat zones.
Below left: The 'Englandblitz' badge of the nightfighters.
Below right: The 'kills' credited to the crews of fighter zone 'Gorilla' by the authorized fighter controller are marked on a propeller blade from a British bomber.

Left: Herbert Lütje (left) and August Geiger (right), receive the Ritterkreuz from Kammhuber, 22 May 1943.

Right: An atmospheric shot of a pilot at the controls of his Ju 88. The angle of lighting and the position of the artificial horizon, apparently 'dead', suggest a staged shot.

Below: NJG 1, stationed at Arnheim, celebrates its third anniversary, 26 June 1943. Anti-clockwise around the table are: Major Ehle of II./NJG 1, unknown, Major Lent of IV./NJG 1, Oberstleutnant Falck, Kommodore NJG 1, Generalmajor Kammhuber, and Major Streib of I./NJG 1.

Daylight Sorties: Senseless Sacrifice

Few episodes in the air defence of the Reich are as indicative of the Luftwaffe's desperation as the use of nightfighters against daylight raiders. The Bf 110 had already shown during the Battle of Britain that it was not much use as a day fighter, and the Bf 110-4 nightfighter, encumbered with heavy electronic gear and the drag-producing 'antlers' of its radar aerial array, was an even less likely candidate for the rôle. However, the type did possess properties which recommended its use against four-engined bombers, particularly its heavy, multiple armament and its long range compared with the Bf 109. Against American escort fighters it had no chance, although some Bf 110 crews were, to everyone's astonishment, able to score against them.

However, in action it was usually the disadvantages which prevailed. Thus on 26 February 1943 Hauptmann Ludwig Becker, the great nightfighting tactician, met his death on his first daylight sortie. The same fate was to overtake many a nightfighter crew, and the loss rate increased as time went by. It is true that an instruction was later issued that only those bombers flying alone were to be attacked, but in the heat of the moment this instruction was usually forgotten. Another difficulty for the night pilots on daylight missions was the fact that they had forgotten, or had never learned, how to attack in the usual Rotte (two-plane) and Schwarm (four-plane) formations. The regular nightfighter tactic of sneaking up alone on the bomber's tail was mostly fatal when tried against the heavily-armed B-17 formations. Although airframe losses were made good relatively easily, the on-board electronics were much harder to replace, and the problem of replacing lost crews was as good as insoluble, for there was no substitute for their experience. The highly-specialized training took a great deal of time—a commodity that was in short supply to the defenders of Germany in 1944, for too much had already been wasted.

Above: A Rotte of Bf 110G-4s from 9./NJG 3 on a daylight sortie against the USAAF. The vapour trails at top left are from bombers of the US Eighth Air Force.
Opposite page, top: A Bf 110G4/R7 climbs to intercept an incoming American bomber formation.
Opposite page, below: American fighters weave around the B-17s in their charge like sheep-dogs around a flock. The slow and unwieldy Bf 110 stood little chance of scoring in the face of such opposition.

This photograph, taken from a B-17, is one of very few to show a Bf 110 in the act of attacking daylight bombers.

A B-17 shot down by a nightfighter, probably flown by Hauptmann Jabs, Commanding Officer of IV./NJG 1, and forced to land on the shore of the Zuider Zee.

Above: Excited discussion after a daylight mission in which, although Hauptmann Jabs scored two victories, German losses were heavy. Right to left: unknown, Jabs, Weissflog, Kuthe; in the background is Jabs's Bf 110.
Below: Jabs demonstrates how he came by his two 'kills'.
Right: P-47 Thunderbolt, probably shot down by Walter Winterhoff during a daylight raid on 30 January 1944.

Left: An artist's impression of a daylight dogfight between a P-51 Mustang and a BF 110; the American fighters were superior in every respect.
Right: On 26 February 1943, 12./NJG 1 lost its Staffelkapitän, Hauptmann Ludwig Becker. This great nightfighting tactician and his radio operator, Oberfeldwebel Staub, were shot down over the North Sea during their first daylight sortie.
Below: Many Bf 110s, such as this one from IV./NJG 1, were shot down during daylight sorties; each experienced crew so sacrificed was a severe loss to the night defence of Germany.

Eyes for the Nightfighter: from 'Spanner' to 'Lichtenstein'

The development and use of electronic search and countermeasures equipment forms an interesting chapter in the history of nightfighting. The lead in developing such electronic aids constantly swung back and forth between Britain and Germany, as they vied with one another for technological supremacy. German engineers, for example, developed FuG (Funkgerät, radio apparatus) 227 Flensburg, to 'home onto' the British tail-warning 'Monica' radar, turning a guardian into a betraying beacon. The first on-board aid installed in German fighters was Spanner (Trouserpress), an optical infra-red seeker device. Leutnant Becker obtained the first victory using FuG 202 (Lichtenstein BC), the earliest on-board radar device. This Lichtenstein equipment and its improved successors, such as SN 2, closed a gap, for the Würzburg-Riese ground radar could not supply coordinates accurate enough to place the fighter in visual contact with its target.

What frequently happened was that the fighter controller brought his charge into the general vicinity of the bomber, but bad visibility or perhaps a new moon prevented the pilot from seeing it. With on-board radar the Bf 110's radio operator could guide the pilot over the last few hundred yards to the target. The Lichtenstein equipment did this by direct radar interrogation of the enemy aircraft, while Naxos homed-on the signals of the British H2S ground-mapping radar, which the Germans knew as Rotterdam from the place where they had first encountered it. British scientists were very resourceful in producing countermeasures against German radar; for instance, they discovered that so simple a device as strips of aluminium foil, cut to a certain length and dropped by the million from aircraft, could blind German radar both on the ground and in the air. This was eventually countered by the German development of a radar which could not be hampered by 'Window', or as the Germans called these foil strips, 'Düppel'.

Thus it continued until the end of the war, a hard-fought struggle to obtain the best electronic equipment. The idea of radar originated in Germany, but thanks to their greater industrial capability and also to faulty planning on the German side, it was the Allies who were able to forge it into a decisive weapon.

Top: The reflector gunsight, used on both day and night fighters, was of limited use at night.

Middle: An early experimental aid was the Spanner infra-red sight, here seen fitted to a Bf 110. The intention was to turn the enemy aircraft's heat emissions into visible light.

Below: The next step was Lichtenstein, the first effective airborne radar. This epoch-making invention gave the Luftwaffe an early and commanding lead in nightfighter development.

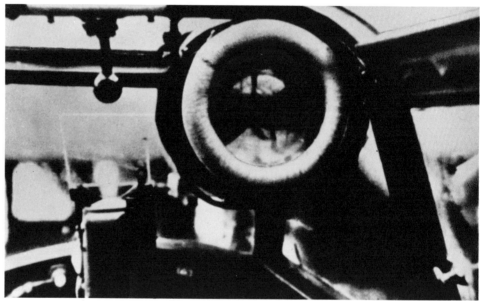

From this angle, the multiple radar antennae and armament make this Bf 110 look like some strange alien monster. The equipment shown here was a development of the Lichtenstein apparatus. The wide-angle FuG 220 radar was based on a marine unit. Also of interest is the under-fuselage pack containing two MG 151 guns; this was rarely fitted to nightfighter aircraft.

Right: Hauptmann Prinz zu Sayn-Wittgenstein was among the more ambitious nightfighter pilots.
Below: Sayn-Wittgenstein's Bf 110 after crashlanding at Venlo, end of 1943.

Right: Oberstleutnant Helm was in charge of the experimental establishment at Werneuchen, where new weapons and equipment were tested and developed for operational use.
Above: Helm often personally tested aircraft fitted with new devices, such as this protective armour plate.
Below: All new or modified types passed through such establishments. Here a new flame-damping exhaust pipe is being tested on a Bf 110.

Radar equipment steadily increased in size, complexity and precision. **Left**: Wassermann M (FuMG 402) long-range radar.
Right: Würzburg-Riese.

Top: Freya-Köthen, with Würzburg-Riese in the background. **Below:** Fighter controllers monitoring the action.

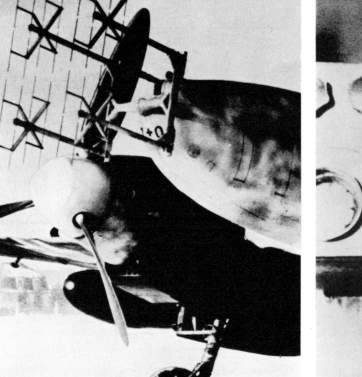

Above left and below: Not only did the radar 'antlers' look clumsy, but they also slowed down the aircraft.

Right: The SN 2 receiver and display unit in the radio operator's position. The screen is inside the padded visor.

156

Left: A group photograph with the fin of Oberleutnant Schnaufer's Bf 110, showing forty-seven victories, as a backdrop. Left to right: Leutnant Matzak, Leutnant Rolland, Oberleutnant Schnaufer and Oberleutnant Weissflog.

Below: The remains of a Lancaster shot down by Oberleutnant Schnaufer near Rischenau, in the district of Höxter, while returning from a raid on Kassel, 22 October 1943. The fuselage is upside down and the bomb bay ceiling is visible, with bomb shackles and boxes for incendiary bombs still attached.

157

Right: Oberstleutnant Helmut Lent, Kommodore of NJG 3, in conversation with Hauptmann Wolfgang Schnaufer, Kommandeur of IV./NJG 1.
Below: Wolfgang Schnaufer prepares for action. The British respectfully dubbed him the 'Phantom of St. Trond'.

Top: A Do 217J in factory finish on its way to the Front.
Middle: The cockpit of a Do 217J. Note that the pilot's seat has been removed.
Below: The nose of a Do 217N, bristling with four MG 17 machine-guns and four MG 151 cannons – truly heavy firepower. Apart from its long range, the armament was all that recommended the Do 217N as a fighter.

Dwindling supplies of raw materials and power, combined with the need to rationalize production, forced constructors to improvize. In order to produce a 'new' nightfighter, the bomber's glazed nose was replaced by a solid one containing guns. In the bomb bay, which retained bomb hangers and doors, Dornier suspended a 300-litre fuel tank. The defensive guns, for which a nightfighter had no use, were removed, along with the dive brakes, yet the all-up weight, especially as electronic gear proliferated, was greater than that of the bomber version. Success was correspondingly limited.

160

Left: After a quarrel with Hitler and Göring, Generalmajor Kammhuber resigned as Inspekteur der Nachtjagd in November 1943. The picture shows the farewell party for the departing nightfighter chief (first from left). Also retiring is Generalleutnant Döring (second from right), leader of one of General 'Beppo' Schmid's fighter divisions. (Schmid is at centre.)
Below: The remaining stock of Do 217Ns went to II./NJG 4.

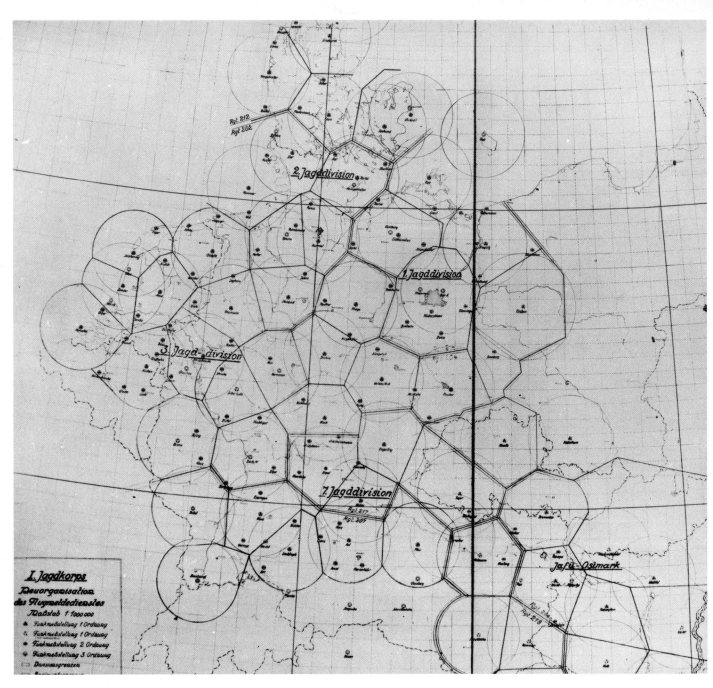

This map of Germany shows the areas for which the various fighter divisions were responsible.

162

Above: Running-up the engines. This Bf 110 still bears the 'shark's mouth' emblem of II./ZG 76.
Right: It is also the ground crew chief's responsibility to ensure that the parachute will function properly should it be needed.
Below: A 110 of NJG 4, again with the Zerstörer 'shark's mouth' markings, about to take off. The wingtip aerials are for the FuG 227 Flensburg equipment, which homes onto the British Monica tail-warning radar.

Top: This Ju 88G-1 of 7./NJG 2, coded 4R + UR, landed in Britain by mistake on 13 July 1944. On board were the latest SN 2 and Flensburg equipment.
Middle: A Ju 88G-6. On this version the underside gondola was deleted to reduce drag.
Below: Schräge Musik – twin oblique upward-firing MG 151/20s on a Ju 88G-7 of NJG 102.

164

Above: A Bf 110 G-4/R3 of 9./NJG 5, summer 1943.
Right: Sorting out the parachute straps could be rather trying at times. The flame-damping exhaust is clearly visible in this view.
Below: While the crew chief helps the skipper to strap in, the radio operator and gunner climb aboard.

Above: Major Eckart-Wilhelm von Bonin commanded II./NJG 1 from 8 November 1943.

The amount of paperwork needed to register a victory is typified in the following example. It concerns one of Hauptmann von Bonin's 'kills'. Bonin first had to file a comprehensive victory claim (right).

Jg./Nachtjagdgeschwader 1 *Auswertung!*   O.U., den 13.6.43.
R.d.L.u.Ob.d.L.L.k., Ag.29 Nr. 1296/44 v.20.12.44 als 7. Lieferung Nr 91.

213

Abschußmeldung

1. Zeit (Tag, Stunde, Minute) und Gegend des Absturzes: 12.6.43.   01.47 Uhr. Oupey
   12 km NO Lüttich/Planquadrat 5141   Höhe: 5700 m

2. Durch wen ist der Abschuß erfolgt: Hptm. von Bonin/Ofw.Johrden

3. Flugzeugtyp des abgeschossenen Flugzeuges: Halifax

4. Staatsangehörigkeit des Gegners: England

   Werknummern bzw. Kennzeichen:

5. Art der Vernichtung:

   a) Flammen mit dunkler Fahne, <u>Flammen mit heller Fahne</u>

   b) Einzelteile weggeflogen, abmontiert (Art der Teile), auseinandergeplatzt

   c) zur Landung gezwungen (diesseits oder jenseits der Front, glatt bzw. mit Bruch)

   d) jenseits der Front am Boden in Brand geschossen

6. Art des Aufschlages (nur wenn dieser beobachtet werden konnte)

   a) <u>diesseits</u> oder jenseits <u>der Front</u>

   b) senkrecht, flachem Winkel, <u>Aufschlagbrand</u>, <u>Staubwolke</u>

   c) nicht beobachtet, warum nicht?

   d) <u>Bruch</u> gefunden

7. Schicksal der Insassen (tot, mit Fallschirm abgesprungen, nicht beobachtet) 1 tot, Rest unbekannt

8. Gefechtsbericht des Schützen ist in der Anlage beigefügt

9. Zeugen: a) Luft Ofw.Johrden (Bordfunker)

             b) Erde Uffz.Bender, Raum 6B (15./Ln.Rgt.211)
             angefasst durch Feldw. Lutz, Fl.H.Kdtr. St.Trond.

10. Anzahl der Angriffe, die auf das feindl. Flugzeug gemacht wurden: 3

11. Richtung, aus der die einzelnen Angriffe erfolgten: hinten-unten und hinten

12. Entfernung, aus der der Abschuß erfolgte: 100 m

13. Takt. Position, aus der der Abschuß angesetzt wurde: von oben

Zu Ziffer 5-7 ist Zutreffendes zu unterstreichen.

Lager-Nr. 1895 Verlag und Druck: Heß, Braunschweig-München

14. Ist einer der feindl. Bordschützen kampfunfähig gemacht worden: unbekannt

15. Verwandte Munitionsart: Mg.151/2o u. Mg.17 - Munition

16. Munitionsverbrauch: Mg.151/2o = 215 Schuß/ Mg.17 = 55o Schuß

17. Art und Anzahl der Waffen, die bei dem Abschuß gebraucht wurden: 4 Mg.151/2o u.4 Mg.17

18. Typ der eigenen Maschine: Bf 110 G4

19. Weiteres taktisch oder technisch Bemerkenswertes: -

20. Treffer in der eigenen Maschine: keine

21. Beteiligung weiterer Einheiten (auch Flak):

    1) Jägerleitoffz. Raum 6 B (Ofw.Kunamann)   15./Ln.Rgt.211
    2) Geräteführer W-Rmot   (Uffz.Loose)   "
    3)   "   W-Blau   (Fw.Bray)   "

Major und Gruppenkommandeur.

von B o n i n , Hptm.
6./N.J.G.1   den 13.6.43.

G e f e c h t s b e r i c h t
_____

zum Dunkelnachtjagdabschuß des Hptm. von Bonin/Ofw.Johrden
am 12.6.43. um ol.47 Uhr.

      Am 12.6.43. startete ich um o.35 Uhr zur Nachtjagd in den Raum 6B. Nach Ansatz erkannte ich gegen ol.4o Uhr ein Feindflugzeug unter mir. Ich setzte mich seitlich ab und ging dann unter das Feindflugzeug,das ich als Halifax ausmachte. Ich schoß aus etwa loo m,worauf die Halifax am rechten Innenmotor schwach und im Rumpf hell brannte. Auf das brennende Flugzeug schoß ich noch zweimal, worauf es senkrecht abstürzte. Den Aufschlag habe ich um ol.47 Uhr beobachtet.

      Der Bruch wurde bei Oupey,12 km NO Lüttich im Planquadrat 5141 gefunden.

II./Nachtjagdgeschwader 1   Gefechtsstand, den 16.6.1943.
-.-.-.-.-.-.-.-.-.-.-.-.-.

Stellungnahme des Gruppenkommandeurs
-.
zum Dunkelnachtjagdabschuß Hptm. von Bonin - Obfw. Johrden
am 12. 6. 1943 um ol.47 Uhr.
-.

Der Abschuß ist einwandfrei.
Besatzung und Erdzeugen sahen den brennenden Absturz und Aufschlag der Feindmaschine.
Der Bruch der Halifax wurde im Dorfe Oupey, 12 km NO Lüttich, gefunden und durch die Meldung des Feldw. Lutz von der Fliegerhorstkommandantur St. Trond bestätigt.
Am Abschuß beteiligt waren Jägerleitoffizier und Gerätebesatzungen des Raumes 6 B von der 15./Ln.-Regt.211.

Major und Gruppenkommandeur.

To this was attached a combat report (top left). Next came an endorsement from the Gruppenkommandeur, Hauptmann Ehle (top right). A second witness, an Unteroffizier from an air intelligence regiment acting as a look-out (below left). To these were added one or more witnesses' reports; below right is that of Oberfeldwebel Johrden, von Bonin's radio operator.

J o h r d e n ,Ofw.
6./N.J.G.1   den 13.6.43.

Z e u g e n b e r i c h t
_____

zum Dunkelnachtjagdabschuß des Hptm.von Bonin/Ofw.Johrden
am 12.6.43. um ol.47 Uhr.

      Am 12.6.43. startete ich um o.35 Uhr mit Hptm. von Bonin als Flugzeugführer zur dunklen Nachtjagd in den Raum 6B. Gegen ol.39 Uhr wurden wir auf ein Feindflugzeug angesetzt. Hptm. von Bonin erkannte das Feindflugzeug unter der eigenen Maschine. Hptm.von Bonin setzte sich seitlich ab und griff dann das Feindflugzeug von unten an. Die Halifax,welche wir als solche erkannten, brannte nach dem ersten Angriff,flog aber weiter. Hptm.von Bonin flog zwei weitere Angriffe,worauf die Halifax brennend,senkrecht abstürzte. Den Aufschlagbrand habe ich um ol.47 Uhr beobachtet.

A b s c h r i f t .

Bender, Herbert   O.U., den 12.6.1943.
Unteroffizier
15./Luftnachrichtenregiment 211.

A u g e n z e u g e n b e r i c h t
zu dem Abschuß am 12.6.1943, ol.47 Uhr im Abschnitt 6 B.

    Am 12.6.1943 war ich bei der Auswertung 6 B als Turmposten eingeteilt. ol.4o Uhr benachrichtigte mich die Auswertung, daß der Jäger in südlicher Richtung berühre. ol.42 Uhr wurde mir als neues Beobachtungsfeld Richtung 4 gegeben. ol.43 Uhr beobachtete ich Feuerwechsel und kurz darauf eine brennende Maschine, die sich noch einige Zeit kurvend in der Luft hielt und ol.47 Uhr mit Explosion auf dem Boden aufschlug.

                       gez. B e n d e r

Für die Richtigkeit der Abschrift:

Hauptmann und Major beim Stabe.

Right: The action is graphically illustrated by this sketch; on this occasion the Red Würzburg (Roter Riese) was tracking the bomber and Blue Würzburg (Blauer Riese) was directing the fighter. The names of the two radar teams are listed, and the different location given for Oupeye (note spelling) is interesting.

Below left: A telegram sent to II./NJG 1 gives details of the whereabouts of the British crew.

Below right: Photographs of the wreck were taken by Air Intelligence Regiment 211 and sent to the Geschwader.

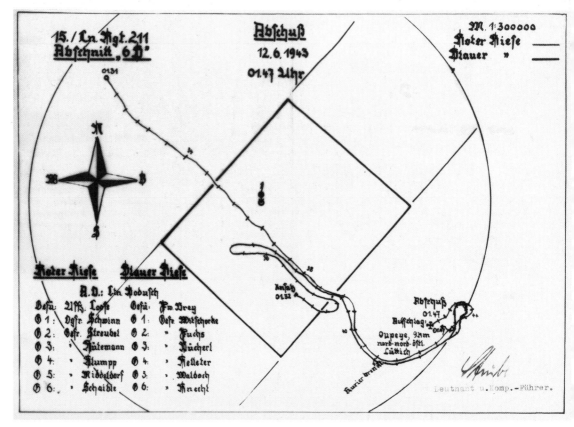

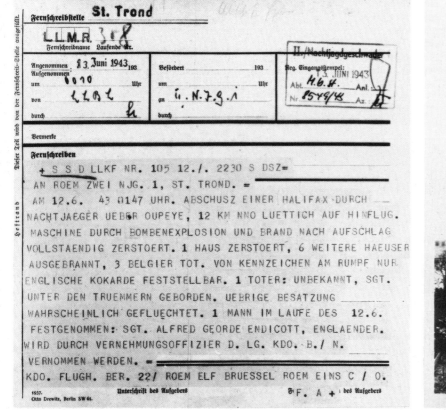

Left: The crew chief, Unteroffizier Ullrich, helps Wolfgang Schnaufer with his straps.
Right: Hauptmann Schnaufer is already in his cockpit, and his radio operator, Leutnant Rumpelhardt, is about to board; behind him is Ullrich.
Below: With engines thundering, Hauptmann Schnaufer's aircraft taxis out to take off.

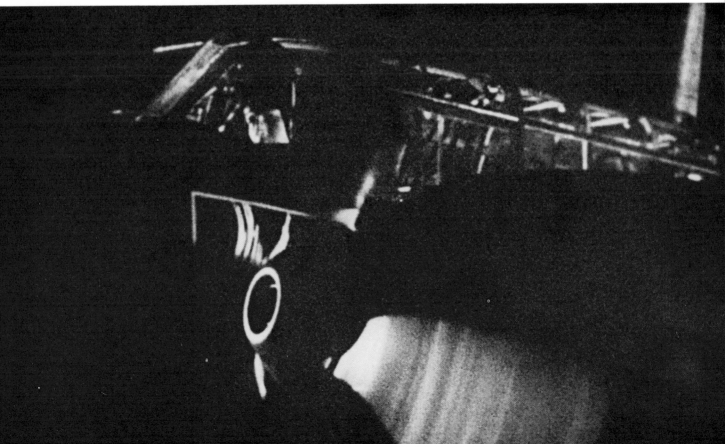

Left: Oberleutnant Leopold Fellerer gives a large audience a graphic description of his latest sortie.
Right: 'Poldi' Fellerer concentrates on his impending take-off on a ferry flight.
Below: Fellerer, Kommandeur of II./NJG 5, with his radio operator Hätscher (left) in front of the fin of his Bf 110 G. Fellerer's score on 14 January 1944, the date of this picture, stood at twenty-two kills.

Above: Whiling away the spare time: a shooting competition at the home of NJG 1 in Deelen. Right to left, Oberleutnant Strüning, Hauptmann von Buchholz, Holzschmitt, a Staff General, Major Vogel, Hauptmann Knickemeyer, Kommodore Oberleutnant Streib, an armaments officer, and Major Hasemann.

Left: Oberleutnant Baake (left) of I/NJG 1, in an introspective game of billiards. On the wall is trophy from a successful sortie.

Right: Did this boxing match between Hans-Joachim Jabs and Helmut Lent count towards the unofficial Luftwaffe championships?

Above: This Bf 110G-4 with Lichtenstein and wing tanks belongs to 6./NJG 6.
Left: Hauptmann Manfred Meurer and his radio operator Oberfeldwebel Scheibe with a fuselage plate from a Lancaster that they shot down. Scheibe was the first radio operator to receive the Ritterkreuz.
Right: An 'old hand' among nightfighters. Oberfeldwebel Wilhelm Beier advises his young comrades on deflection shooting.

Right: Schnaufer's crew preparing for action. While Wolfgang Schnaufer waves to the camera, Rumpelhardt, the radio operator, struggles with his parachute.
Below: This Wellington, which was forced down during the night, crash-landed and burned out on the airfield at St. Trond.

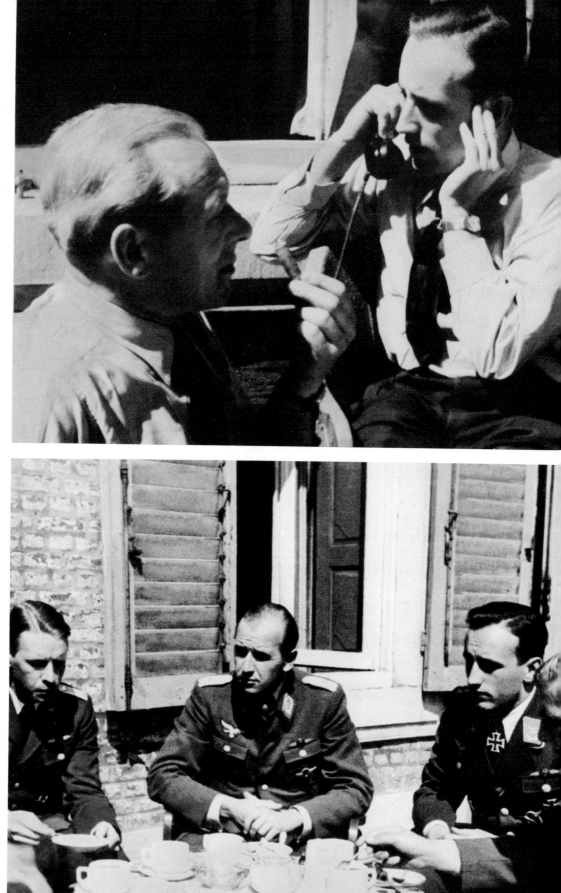

Top: While Wolfgang Schnaufer appears to be having trouble with a poor line, Major Rotter sniffs at his cigar.
Below: The Kommodore, Oberstleutnant Streib, takes coffee with his officers; left to right, Oberleutnant Greiner, Streib, Oberleutnant Schnaufer, and Oberleutnant Weissflog.

174

Geheim

Geheime Kommandosache

Angenommen
Aufgenommen

Datum: 28.3. 19 44

um: 16 Uhr

von: L6.15V

durch: Pros

Befördert:

Datum: 19

um: MRZ Uhr

an: 1129% 44

durch:

Rolle:

Vermerke:

-- G E H E I M --

Fernschreiben

KR LBKV 01488 28/3. (1445).=

AN HERRN HPTM. HANS JOACHIM JABS, KDR. ROEM VIER. NJG 1

EBER LFL. KDO. REICH.=

LIEBER JABS.- ZU DER HOHEN TAPFERKEITSAUSZEICHNUNG

PRECHE ICH IHNEN GLUECKWUNSCH UND ANERKENNUNG FUER IHRE

ORBILDLICHEN LEISTUNGEN AUS. DER ERBITTERTE KAMPF DER

EUTSCHEN NACHTJAEGER GEGEN DIE FEINDLICHEN TERRORVERBAENDE

AND IN DER VERLEIHUNG DES EICHENLAUBS ZUM RITTERKREUZ

ES EISERNEN KREUZES AN SIE, ALS KOMMANDEUR EINER

KAMPFBEWAEHRTEN NACHTJAGDGRUPPE, EINE ERNEUTE WUERDIGUNG .

Nicht zu übermitteln:

RC Unterschrift des Aufgebers

Fernsprech-Anschluß des Aufgebers

r-Nr. 1578a. Verlag und Druck Heß, Braunschweig-München. 32.6. 40. 100 000

RCH DEN FUEHRER. MOEGE IHNEN DAS SOLDATENGLUECK

EU SEIN.=

GOERING REICHSMARSCHALLL DES GROSZDEUTSCHEN REICHES UND

OBERBEFEHLSHABER DER LUFTWAFFE .

A congratulatory telegram from Luftwaffe C-in-C Göring to Hauptmann Hans-Joachim Jabs on the award of Oak Leaves to his Knight's Cross.

Top: Sceptical faces.
Below: Awards ceremony at Obersalzburg, 24 April 1944. Hautpmann Jabs is next in line to receive Oak Leaves to his Knight's Cross; left to right, Kurt Bühlingen, Jabs, Bernhard Jope, Hansgeorg Bätcher, Adolf Hitler and Reinhard Seiler.

176

Top: Three of the most successful German nightfighter pilots break for coffee; left to right, Major Lent, Oberleutnant Schnaufer and a thoughtful Major Jabs.
Middle: By 1944 even non-radar equipped Bf 110s were in use as nightfighters.
Below: Oberleutnant Schnaufer and Major Jabs examine a P-47 Thunderbolt shot down by flak while attacking the airfield at low level. At left is Leutnant Milius.

Left: The Kommodore of NJG 1, Major Jabs, leaves his Bf 110.
Right: He is greeted by the Kommandeur of IV./NJG 1, Oberleutnant Schnaufer, whose Gruppe he is visiting.
Below: Another guest: General Grabmann has arrived in his Siebel Sh 104.

178

Top: This Ju 88R-2 still has the ventral gondola of the original bomber version, which was retained on the early nightfighters. The gondola was fitted with extra armament.
Middle: A Ju 88G-1 coded R4+JK, and thus from 2./NJG 2, on a ferry flight.
Below: This Ju 88R-1, Work Number 360043, landed at Dyce in Scotland on 9 May 1943. The crew, led by Oberleutnant Schmidt of 11./NJG 3, had previously arranged their defection with British Intelligence, and the aircraft yielded valuable information. It is now on display at the Battle of Britain Museum, Hendon.

179

Top: The château at St. Trond by-and-by came to house the élite of the German nightfighter command.
Middle: Hans-Joachim Jabs and Hermann Greiner outside the château.
Below: Happy faces: left to right, Weissflog, Grabmann, Schnaufer and Jabs.

180

Left: Discussing the situation with Air Fleet Reich commander Generaloberst Stumpff. At left is his assistant, Oberst Falck.
Below, right: Enemy flights were reported to the night-fighter control centres by the flight reporting stations using this grid system. The message "enemy bomber flight in plan square Theodor-Cäsar" thus meant that the bombers were over Nuremberg.

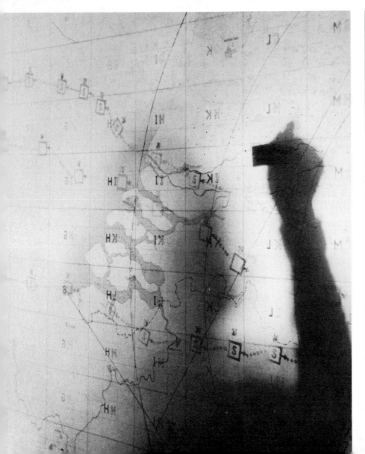

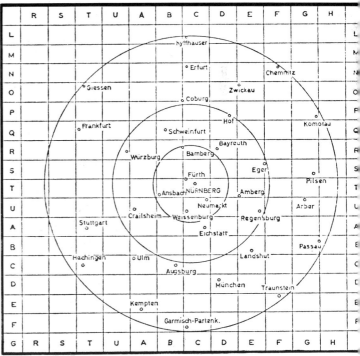

Left: This is how it looked in practice. The course of the enemy and the positions of the defending fighters were drawn on the frosted glass screen.

Top: At dusk final preparations are made for action.
Middle: A British bomber breaks up in flames after a direct hit.
Below: What remains of the bomber is found next morning. (Translator's note: This is a Boston, used as a day bomber.)

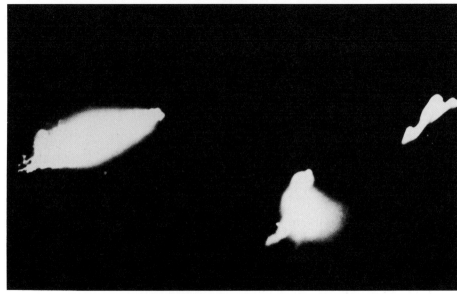

182

The 'Wild Boar'

One of the many new ideas calculated to give the 'defenders of the Reich' a much-needed boost and some equally necessary relief came from former fighter pilot Major Hajo Herrmann. He suggested using single-engined day fighters at night; these would climb above the British bombers, which, silhouetted by flak searchlights from below, would then be an easy target. This would enable the Bf 109 and Fw 190 to attack as in daylight. After successful trials with a test unit, Major Herrmann established JG 300 on 26 June 1943. Other units soon followed. The 'wilde Sau', as this system and its associated Geschwader were called, lived up to its name, creating havoc like the proverbial wild boar among the enemy. However, it caused less confusion among the British bombers than among the defenders; soon no-one in the operations rooms knew who was friend or foe. Furthermore, the single-engined aircraft were not well suited to blind-flying, and their pilots, most of whom had no experience of flying on instruments, succumbed in large numbers to take-off and landing accidents. So the 'wild boar' returned to daylight operations.

Left: Dramatic impression of a 'wild boar' Bf 109G in action, with the 'wilde Sau' emblem at centre.
Right: Oberst Herrmann invented the 'wild boar' system. Herrmann, who came to fighters from the bomber arm, formed the first Geschwader to use the new technique, JG 300.
Below: The Bf 109 aircraft were transferred from day to nightfighting. This move caused great problems, as the aircraft were not equipped, nor were the pilots trained, for night flying.

Top: A British Pathfinder (left) releases his flares over a German town to act as markers for the following raiders. The white clouds around the bomber at right are flak bursts.
Middle: A Bf 109 is prepared for a night sortie.
Below: Leutnant Kraft flew 'wilde Sau' missions with 7./JG 300. Here he is with his Bf 109G-10/R2.

185

Top: Göring visits single-engined night-fighter units. He is greeted by Herrmann, who was then Inspector of Air Defence.

Middle: Hermann Göring in conversation with nightfighter commanders; at centre is Major Radusch.

Below: Generalleutnant Josef Schmid, here visiting a 'wilde Sau' unit, succeeded Kammhuber as leader of I. Fighter Corps from September 1943.

186

Bf 109G-6 nightfighters were even deployed in the far north. A section of JG 302 was stationed for a while in Helsinki.

Hauptmann Müller, also known as 'Nasenmüller' ('Nosey Miller'), was the most successful 'wild boar' pilot, with twenty-three kills from fifty-two sorties.

Top: An Fw 190A-5 of 1./NJGr. 10 was experimentally fitted at Werneuchen with a FuG 217 Neptun, a rear-warning radar.
Middle: Oberleutnant Krause, the pilot, rolls himself a well-earned cigarette.
Below: 'Jllo' was the abbreviation for Jägerleitoffizier (fighter controller). Which of those worthies was identified with this 'wild boar' insignia?
Opposite page, top: An Fw 190, with underwing fuel tanks to extend its range, revs-up prior to departure.
Below: A pilot of Nachtjagdkommando Fw 190, returning from a successful sortie, is congratulated by one of his squadron-mates. This unit was stationed at Aalborg in 1943.

188

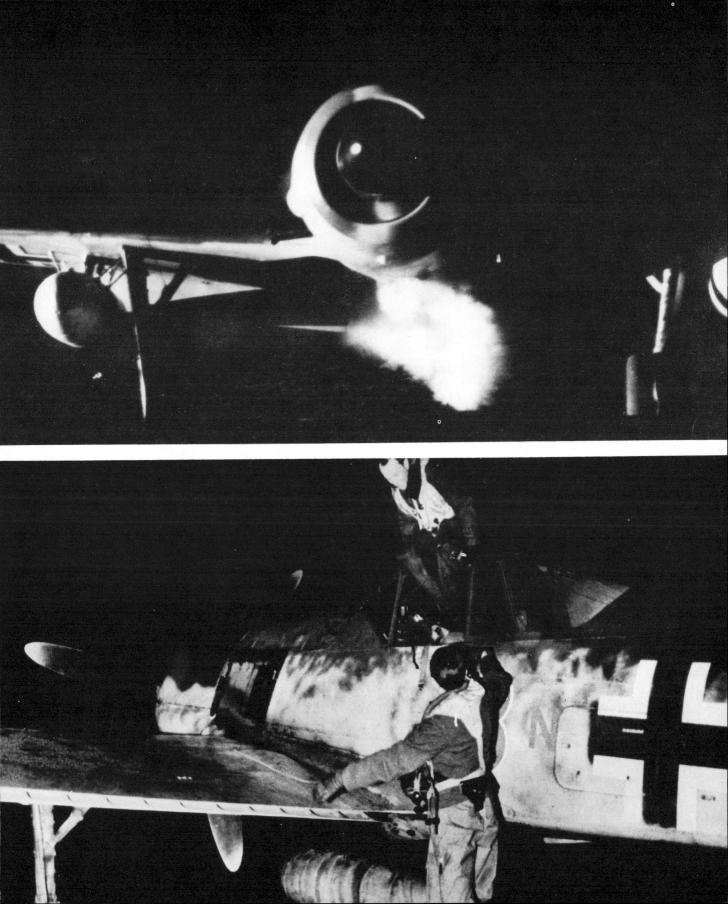

New Hopes

British raids of increasing frequency and by ever-greater numbers of aircraft, coupled with the large-scale introduction of the Mosquito long-range nightfighter, posed severe problems for the Bf 110- and Ju 88-equipped Nachtjagdgeschwader. German aircraft used as nightfighters so far had simply been modified versions of long-range fighters (Zerstörer) or bombers; no types specially designed for night combat were available. Apart from the Bf 110, such machines as the Ju 88, Do 17, Do 215 and 217 had never been intended for any kind of fighter rôle. The RLM's (Reichsluftministerium or Air Ministry) reluctance to commission the development of a purpose-built nightfighter was due on the one hand to the belief that the war would soon be over, and on the other to the fear of teething troubles delaying the production and entry into effective service of any new type. It followed, therefore, that any encouraging develop-

ments, such as the He 219, which, apart from some initial problems, fulfilled many of the requirements of a good nightfighter, were not put into production. The Me 262b might have brought some relief from the depredation of the British long-range fighters, but, for reasons which were partly technical, did not enter large-scale service. The Ar 243, another jet, had an extensively glazed flight-deck, which disqualified it on the grounds that the pilot would be too exposed to injury from aircraft wreckage or shell fragments. A further alternative was the Ta 154, but this machine was having problems with ersatz adhesives used in its construction; an additional drawback was the fuselage, which was too narrow to carry the necessary electronic gear. The development of high-performance nightfighters such as the Do 335 and Ju 388, as well as the Ta 154, did not progress beyond the initial stages. Plotting and scheming among the interested aircraft firms, an unfathomable evaluation policy at the RLM, and a lack of technical foresight, all did more than their share to hinder the urgently needed re-equipment of the nightfighter units, while Germany's towns were bombed into ashes and rubble and many hundreds of thousands were killed.

In this way the newly-raised hopes of the nightfighter crews were dashed once more.

Lack of insight into the necessities of a highly technical war ensured that the Luftwaffe lost the initiative. It should not be left unsaid that, Göring and Milch, as those responsible, bore a large part of the blame. Their inability to get Hitler to consider vital issues, and to carry worthwhile ideas through, was a prime cause of the failure of the Luftwaffe, and with it the nightfighter arm.

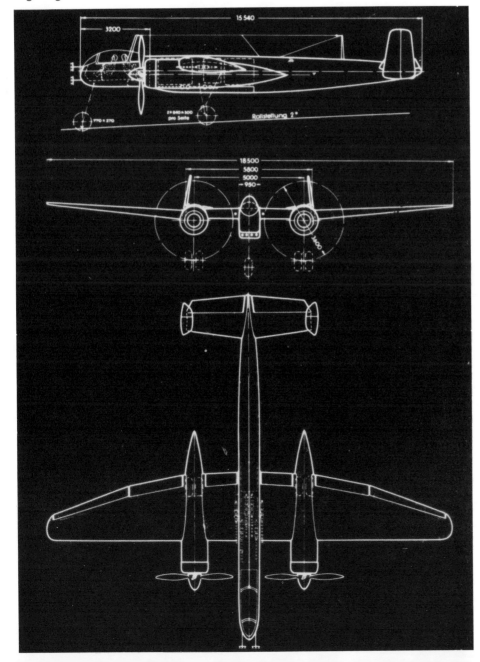

Plan, front and side elevations of the He 219 'Uhu', which was already on the drawing-board when Heinkel began development of a machine specially suited to night-fighting.

Opposite page, top: Although described as a wind-tunnel model, this looks remarkably like a real prototype He 219.

Opposite page, below: The He 219 prototype was built with sockets to take the aerials associated with SN 2 radar.

Top: The cockpit of the He 219; the use of compact side consoles saved space and weight.

Middle: Right-hand side of pilot's cockpit; at left are three fuel gauges.

Below: Right-hand side (port) of the rearward facing radio operator's cockpit. The oxygen regulators are prominent in this and the preceding photograph.

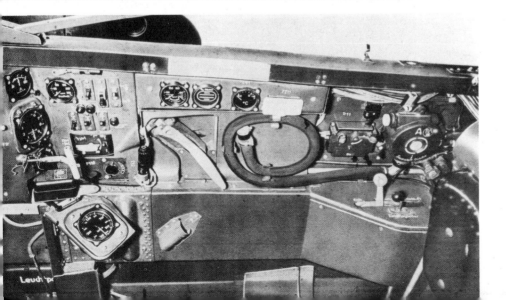

193

Top: The He 219 was Germany's first purpose-built nightfighter, a viable alternative to the earlier improvised types.

Middle: This new nightfighter demonstrated substantially better qualities than the Bf 110 and Ju 88. It even managed to catch and bring down several of the hitherto invulnerable Mosquito long-range nightfighters.

Below: SN 2 antennae on an He 219A-7. The Roman figure 'VI' indicates that the FuG 220d version of Lichtenstein is fitted. This is also disclosed by the diagonally-mounted dipole aerials.

Above: Oberstleutnant Werner Streib's He 219. Note the retractable crew ladder.
Below: Streib really put this new machine to the test on the night of 11-12 June 1943, when he managed to shoot down five British aircraft.

To finish his night of triumph, Oberstleutnant Streib crashed on landing owing to instrument failure and a faulty flap lock. Streib was unhurt, but radio operator Fischer broke both legs. The Reichsluftministerium seized upon this unfortunate accident as an excuse for not ordering the otherwise outstanding He 219 into production. This was a grave mistake, for the advantages of this machine far outweighed its teething troubles.

The Me 262 was also evaluated as a nightfighter, initially as a single-seater then in the fully-fledged night version as a two-seater. However, the 262B-1a, like its day fighter equivalent, was not ordered into worthwhile production until too late, and saw little service.

Top: Fighter pilots in serious mood. This picture was taken near Bremen at the end of 1944, at a demonstration of new fighter aircraft; left to right, General der Jagdflieger Galland (General Commanding, Fighter Arm), Oberstleutnant Streib, Inspeckteur der Nachtjäger (Inspector of Nightfighters), Professor Tank, designer of the Fw 190, Ta 154 and several other successful types, and Oberst Trautloft, Superintendent East on Galland's staff.
Middle: Major Schönert's Ju 88G-6 with vertical arrangement of SN 2 aerials. The rear warning radar aerials protruded horizontally from the fin.
Below: A Ju 88G-6 of NJG 5. The antennae on the fin are for the FuG 218 Neptun rear-warning radar.

198

The Ta 154 was a wooden twin-engined fighter which failed to enter production because of a shortage of the special adhesive developed for it; no workable substitute could be found.

The Last Victories

Simultaneously with the greatly increased American daylight raids, the RAF stepped up its nightly onslaught. As the Germans withdrew from the formerly occupied territories in the West, the nightfighters lost their bases outside Germany, the westerly and Dutch coastal radar stations, and several controlled zones. This allowed the enemy bombers to approach much nearer before detection, and forced nightfighter divisional staffs to improvise. The crews in their machines were faced with a situation similar to that of years previously, of having to rely on their wits and experience. Yet despite all difficulties, crews continued to score; this is all the more remarkable in view of the dwindling facilities and the lack of complete training of replacement airmen. Also noteworthy was the growing success rate of British night intruders in downing German nightfighters engaged in taking-off and landing; here was another idea of German origin, abandoned through Hitler's narrowness of outlook, now coming home to roost.

Top: Night after night the British bombers attacked German towns. This photograph was taken during a raid on Hamburg. The wavy lines are the tracks of tracer ammunition from light flak, distorted by camera vibration.
Middle: Yet another nightfighter victory, this time near den Helder.
Below: Thirteen victories on the fin of Hauptmann Breves's Bf 110 of NJG 1. Breves shot down twelve four-engined bombers and a Mosquito.

Top: Despite the increasing severity of the battle and the accompanying losses, the Kommandeure of NJG 1 do not appear to have lost any of their customary cheerfulness and optimism. Left to right: Oberleutnant Weissflog; Major Schnaufer, Kommandeur IV./NJG 1; Major Drewes, Kommandeur III./NJG 1; Major Sutor; Oberstleutnant Jabs, Kommodore NJG 1; Hauptmann Dormann of the Geschwader staff; Major Förster, Kommandeur I./NJG 1; Major von Bonin, Kommandeur II./NJG 1; Hauptmann Knickemeyer, Geschwader armament officer, and, on the ground, Hauptmann Greiner, Staffelkapitän of 12./NJG 1.

Middle: Aces in conference; left to right, Hauptmann Schnaufer, Hauptmann Breves, Hauptmann Augenstein with bandage, and Hauptmann Greiner.

Below: Out for a stroll in Deelen.

202

Top: A successful nightfighter pilot receives the Eichenlaub zum Ritterkreuz des Eisernen Kreuzes (Oak Leaves to the Knight's Cross to the Iron Cross). Major Prinz zu Sayn-Wittgenstein's investiture was in September 1943; to his left is fighter pilot Major Grasser, to the right Hauptmann Rall, who received the Swords to his Ritterkreuz.
Middle: Nightfighters were carefully camouflaged during the day to protect them from Allied ground-attack aircraft.
Below: IV./NJG 1 aircrew at readiness dine in their full uniform and life jackets; second from left, with Ritterkreuz, is Oberfeldwebel Vinke.

203

These muzzle flash dampers were one of many new modifications that gradually improved the nightfighters' effectiveness.

The almost vertical MK 108 cannon and the MG 81 Z free machine-gun made for a cramped rear cockpit in this Bf 110.

Shortly before coming in to land at Deelen on 29 April 1944, after a ferry flight from St. Trond, Major Jabs spotted six single-engined fighters circling above the airfield. Initially he assumed that they were German, but as they turned towards him and his wingman he recognized them as Spitfires. Jabs's only form of defence was attack. The Spitfires dived on the nightfighter at a shallow angle in a head-on attack; Major Jabs opened fire with his heavy cannons and machine-guns, and hit two of the six Spitfires, forcing them to land. Jabs's aircraft was also hit and he too was forced down when the rest of the British flight, from 132 Squadron, attacked him. The leader of the British unit was the well-known ace Squadron Leader Geoffrey Page, DSO, DFC and Bar. Jabs is seen here inspecting the Spitfire Mk IXB flown by Flying Officer John Coulton, a New Zealander.

Bitte, dem
Gefangenen diesen
Zettel als Anden-
ken an Major
Jabs zu lassen.

MAJOR
JABS

29. 4. 44

ABSCHUSS UM 13.00 UHR BEI
SLUK-ENUK, 7km NW. NIJMEGEN

Major Jabs gave Coulton this piece of paper to take with him into captivity; it would have unexpected repercussions. The message reads: 'Please allow the prisoner to keep this note as a reminder of Major Jabs. Shot down at 13.00 hrs near Sluk-Enuk, 7km NW of Nijmegen'.
Opposite page: Twenty-six years after this dramatic meeting, a Lüdenscheid local paper reported the reunion of the two former opponents. John Coulton, who now lives in New Zealand with his British wife and manufactures ice cream, managed to patiently track down his victor with the help of his daughter, who was working as a nurse in England. Major Jabs's slip of paper and the photograph at top right were the key to a new-found international friendship. (After leaving Deelen, Coulton had been taken to Frankfurt for interrogation, then to a camp, Stalag Luft III. He received hospital treatment at Obermassfeld, returned to Luft III, and was subsequently transferred to Nuremberg and Moosberg before his release.)

Nach 26 Jahren ein Brief vom ehemaligen Gegner

John Caulton aus Neuseeland schrieb an Hans-Joachim Jabs, der ihn 1944 abschoß – Besuch in Aussicht gestellt

Lüdenscheid. Vor wenigen Tagen erhielt Herr Hans-Joachim Jabs aus Lüdenscheid, Peterstraße 22, einen Brief, der einen weiten Weg hinter sich hatte. Er kam aus Neuseeland, also von der anderen Seite unserer Erdkugel. Ihr Inhalt mußte Empfänger in Erstaunen setzen, und er führte Jabs in der Erinnerung um mehr 6 Jahre zurück, mitten in die zerstrittene und kriegerische Welt von 1944.

war am 29. April. Hans-Joachim Jabs damals Oberstleutnant und Kommodeu des Nachtjagdgeschwaders 1 in Arnheim (Holland). Er kam von einer Besichtigung der 3. Gruppe zurück (eine Gruppe damals die größte fliegende Einheit der Luftwaffe). Es war noch Tag, und er von St. Trond in Belgien auf Arnheim zu. diesem Tag waren starke Anflüge von Amerikaner mit Jägerbegleitung ins erfolgt.

ÜBER DEM PLATZ

Jabs im Tiefflug in die Gegend von Arnheim kam, sah er über dem Flugplatz einige Jäger kreisen. Er hielt sie für deutsche Maschinen, die von der Verfolgung der Amerikaner zurückgekommen waren. Jabs selbst flog eine zweirige ME-110-Nachtjagdmaschine, die so schnell wie die Jäger war, daß sie sich mit englischen und amerikanischen Jagdmaschinen nicht messen

dann ging alles sehr schnell. Als auf den Platz zuflog, erkannte er in kreisenden Jägern sechs moderne ..res, mit Bordkanonen und MGs bestückt. Ein Ausweichen war nicht mehr möglich. Auch hatten die Gegner bereits deutsche Maschine erkannt. Er eröffnete deshalb sofort das Feuer. Er traf Maschine des britischen Oberleutnants Caulton, der aus Neuseeland ..r Nähe des Flugplatzes niederging ..te. Übrigens schoß Jabs in diesem ..kampf noch eine zweite Spitfire ab, doch auch seine eigene Maschine wurde getroffen, und explodierte auf dem Boden ..em mit seiner Besatzung noch gerade

..TERLICHER GEGNER

..r englische Oberleutnant John Caulnur leicht verwundet, wurde von Jabs Fliegerhorst mitgenommen und gut ..orgt. In die Gefangenschaft gab ihm ..ein Schreiben mit der Anweisung ..den ritterlichen Gegner gut zu be..lein.

..bgeschossene Spitfire auf dem Flugplatz von Arnheim

Soweit die Erinnerung an den 29. April 1944. Und nun der Brief aus Neuseeland vom Oktober 1970:

Sehr geehrter Herr Jabs,

Sie werden zweifellos sehr erstaunt sein, diesen Brief von mir zu bekommen. Während der letzten 26 Jahre habe ich mich oft gefragt, ob Sie den Krieg wohl überlebt haben, und wie es Ihnen wohl ergangen sein mag. Dann gingen jedoch sehr vereinzelt Nachrichten über Sie bei mir ein, indem ich Ihren Namen in verschiedenen Büchern erwähnt fand.

Kürzlich machte meine älteste Tochter einen Arbeits-Urlaub in England und erfuhr über meinen Schwager, der zur Zeit bei der Royal Air Force dient, mittels einer Anfrage bei Ihrem Konsulat in England, daß Sie den Krieg überlebt haben und wohlauf sind.

Darf ich Ihre Erinnerung an jenen Tag 1944 nochmals auffrischen . . . ich flog eine SPITFIRE IX B Schwadron-Markierung FF-G, als ich in der Nähe von Nijmegen einen „head-on encounter" (Luftkampf) mit Ihnen hatte, auf Grund dessen ich für ein Jahr in Kriegsgefangenschaft geriet.

Ich füge diesem Schreiben eine „Kopie der Erinnerungs-Unterschrift bei, die Sie mir an diesem Nachmittag gaben. Das Original davon habe ich ebenfalls noch zusammen mit unserem gemeinsamen Photo, das an diesem Tag auch gemacht wurde.

Nach diesem Tage kam ich über Amsterdam nach Frankfurt (Vernehmung), dann nach Aachen (?) (Luft III), später nach Obermaßfeld (Krankenhaus); dann zurück nach Aachen und später nach Nürnberg und Moosberg.

Nach meiner Rückkehr nach Hause habe ich geheiratet, und ca. ein Jahr lang weiter geflogen. Dann habe ich mich dazu entschlossen, nach Neuseeland zurückzukehren und bin aus der Air Force ausgeschieden.

Während der letzten 21 Jahre habe ich mich mit der Herstellung von Speiseeis selbständig gemacht. Ich habe drei Kinder, die 23, 21 und 18 Jahre alt sind. Till,

meine älteste Tochter, sie ist 23 Jahre, arbeitet als ausgebildete Krankenschwester in England, ist gerade von einer ausgedehnten Europareise zurückgekehrt. Ich hätte Sie sicherlich aufgesucht, wenn wir Ihre Anschrift gehabt hätten, denn sie ist von der Schweiz quer durch Deutschland nach Holland gefahren.

Ich habe meiner Familie oft von Ihrem vorbildlichen Verhalten an jenem Tage 1944 in der für mich sehr gefährlichen Situation erzählt.

Till kommt nach Neuseeland noch vor Weihnachten dieses Jahres zurück. Meine Frau und ich hoffen in ca. 18 Monaten eine Überseereise nach England und Europa machen zu können, und ich würde Sie dann gern unter etwas glücklicheren Umständen als damals wiedersehen.

Haben Sie vielleicht mal an Treffen der GAF oder RAF teilgenommen? Dann könnte es möglich sein, daß Sie meinen früheren Commander, Wing Commander Allen Geoffrey Page D. S. O., D. F. C & Bar kennengelernt haben. Mein Freund Geoffrey ist während der Schlacht um England abgeschossen worden und hat sehr schwere Brandverletzungen davongetragen. Er lebt zur Zeit in Genf. Wir flogen an dem Tag unseres Zusammentreffens zusammen.

Ich muß mich entschuldigen, daß ich Ihnen Englisch schreibe, aber mein Deutsch ist doch zu begrenzt. Ich erinnere mich jedoch, daß Sie bei unserem Zusammentreffen ausgezeichnet Englisch sprachen.

Ich schließe diesen Brief nun in der Hoffnung, daß Sie die Zeit finden werden, mir zu antworten, um mir einiges aus Ihrem Leben und Erfahrungen aus den letzten 26 Jahren zu berichten.

Mit freundlichen Grüßen
Ihr John Caulton

BAND UM DEN ERDBALL

So ein Brief bereitet Freude eigener Art, das wissen wir. Er bestätigt, daß auch in der Welt von 1944, in der allein der Haß zu regieren schien, noch Anstand und Ritterlichkeit auch bei Gegner etwas galten. Sie gelten auch heute soviel, daß sie nach 26 Jahren noch ein Band um den halben Erdball zu knüpfen vermögen.

Am 29. April 1944: Oberstleutnant Jabs (links) im Gespräch mit dem von ihm abgeschossenen RAF-Oberleut..

Der deutsche Soldat des Zweiten Weltkrieges hat es in der Nachkriegszeit schwer gehabt. Man hat ihn für die Übergriffe einzelner büßen lassen, obwohl in einem Krieg keine Seite ganz ohne Schuld bleiben kann. Aber der deutsche Soldat schien in der ganzen Welt verfemt, und

auch im Nachkriegs-Deutschland selbst haben ihn bestimmte Kreise gar zu gern verächtlich gemacht.

VON AMERIKANERN GEEHRT

Unter diesen Aspekten gilt ein Brief wie der oben veröffentlichte viel. Übrigens versagt der ehemalige Gegner dem deutschen Soldaten die Anerkennung nicht. So wurden zum Beispiel mit Jabs zusammen der ehemalige Inspekteur der Luftwaffe, Streib, und Oberst Falk, Geschwader-Kommodore der Nachtjagd und Vorgänger von Jabs, von der amerikanischen „Nightfighter Association" zu Ehrenmitgliedern ernannt. Die Ehrung wurde von dem früheren Befehlshaber der US Army Air Force, General Spaatz, vorgenommen. Die Ehrenurkunden wur-

den den ausgezeichne.. ..tige Luftwaffe zugestellt

So kann man hoffen, ..schaft von ihrem weitgel.. ist. Jedenfalls erwartet .. Jabs mit herzlichen Gef.. ..raden mit den anderen ..

Stadtmeisterschaft..

Lüdenscheid. In Kü.. diesjährigen Kegel-St.. an der sich alle Ke.. Kreis beteiligen kön.. ..chung ist am Donner.. tober, um 20 Uhr in .. Da die Vorrunde bis .. abgeschlossen sein soll.. gebeten, ihre Anmeld.. Einzelmeisterschaft zu ..

geben, so daß sofort .. ..chung der Termin-.. stellt werden kann. .. heißt es in der Keg.. Stadtmeisterschaften, f .. ..bellensystem bei Hin.. unter Beisitz eines .. ters statt. Bei jedem .. „die Holz der fünf bes.. tet. Die Hälfte der te.. mit den niedrigsten H.. und Rückkampf schei.. ..lichen Clubs bestreiten .. nach den gleichen Rege.. Clubs mit der höchst.. Zwischenrunde bestr.. auf einer neutralen D.. Paarung zu den einze.. scheidet das Los."

Schwerer Sa..

Lüdenscheid. In d.. fuhr in der Mozartst.. einen parkenden Pkw .. sitzende Fahrer wurd.. Krankenhaus ambula.. nach vorn geschobene .. einem wegen Gegen.. Pkw zusammen. Es .. Sachschaden.

Above: Wolfgang Schnaufer, top nightfighter pilot, and 'Bubi' Hartmann, the foremost day-fighter ace, receive the Swords to their Knights' Crosses from Hitler at his headquarters, the Wolfsschanze (Wolf's Lair).

Left: Hauptmann Drewes congratulates Schnaufer on his one hundredth victory. In the background is Helmut Lent.

Below: After the 'Swords' investiture Schnaufer gets a real live 'lucky swine' from his comrades; left to right, Drewes, Leutnant Gräfe, Staff Medical Officer Dr. Schreiber, Schnaufer and Major Rotter.

Top: Wolfgang Schnaufer joins his radio operator Rumpelhardt and some mechanics for a group portrait in front of a Do 215 on the airfield at Dortmund in October 1944.
Middle: A successful crew: Oberfeldwebel Gänseler, Hauptmann Schnaufer and Leutnant Rumpelhardt.
Below: How does the 'gong' look on Wilhelm Gänseler?

Above: Two Bf 110G-4s of NJG 3 on an airfield near the German border.
Left: The Lichtenstein SN 2 antennae give an aircraft the appearance of a gigantic insect.
Below: These 'insects' can sting, too, as this wrecked Halifax testifies. It was shot down at 2.40am on 26 June 1943 near Zand, 13km south of den Helder.

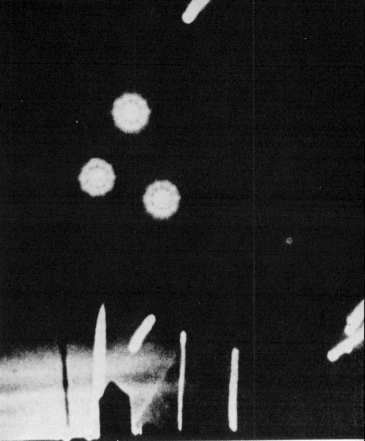

Left: Intense concentration clearly shows on the face of this nightfighter pilot as he scans the night sky.
Right: Rocket flares and flak bursts point the way to the bomber stream.
Below: A single nightfighter sets off at dusk to engage a selected opponent.

Above: The Gruppe on parade before the Château Marchais. Generalmajor Junck thanks the men for their outstanding work.
Left: The General commanding 3. Jagdkorps, Generalmajor Junck, visits III./NJG 1 at Laon Athies on 12 May 1944. He is received by Hauptmann Martin Drewes.
Below: Generalmajor Junck talking to the Gruppe's Adjutant, Leutnant Walter Scheel, who was President of the Federal Republic at the time of writing. Left to right, Oberleutnant Willy Menger, Oberleutnant Pfaff, Oberfeldwebel Georg Petz, Scheel, Hauptmann Drewes (back to camera) and Generalmajor Junck.

Der Kommandeur,
Oh, quelle malheur,
Hat keine passende Mütze mehr.

Die schönste aus seinem Mützenreiche,
Die gänzlich vergammelte weiche,
Verbrannte in der „Kalten Eiche".

Die Gattin hörte es voll Schreck.
„Die schönste Deiner Mützen weg? —
Die war doch gerade so keck!"

Zum Wiegenfeste in Erregung
Setzt sich einer in Bewegung,
Kauft 'ne neue Kopfbedegung.

Es legt die Hand
An den Mützenrand
Der Adjutant.

20. 10. 1944

Scheel, Leutnant

Die Mütze

A little joke between Adjutant and Kommandeur. The poem cannot be done justice in translation, but it tells the sad story of how the Kommandeur's best cap was burnt to ashes in a local hostelry. We can only guess at the identity of the arsonist!

Major Wilhelm Herget came to night-fighting from a Zerstörer unit with fourteen kills to his credit, and went on to become one of the foremost exponents of nightfighting. Despite, or largely because of, his short stature, 'der Kleine' ('Tich'), as his men affectionately called him, set an example for all.

Top: Major Herget at debriefing.

Middle: As Kommandeur of I./NJG 4, Herget invests successful crews with the Iron Cross Second Class.

Below: Snack in hand, Herget listens to the controller directing one of his fighters towards the enemy.

Left: This time Hauptmann Drewes and his radio operator Oberfeldwebel Petz have come a cropper. The freshly doctored pair leave the sick bay at Leuwarden, 24 July 1944.
Right: Oberleutnant Grobe from the Propaganda Corps wants to know exactly what happened.
Below: Nightfighter schools attempted to counter the rising losses with accelerated training. Some schools did not even have radar sets with which to train radio operators.

Top: As the British bomber streams fly across Germany, their path is anxiously followed by the Staffelkapitäne of II./NJG 4. Some, like the pilot on the right, wear dark glasses indoors so as not to impair their night vision.
Middle: Parachute flares guide the bombers to the blacked-out towns.
Below: After the raid the German cities were brilliantly illuminated by fires. The RAF intensified its attacks on residential districts from the beginning of 1944 after a regrettable order from the Chief of Bomber Command, Air Marshal Harris.

216

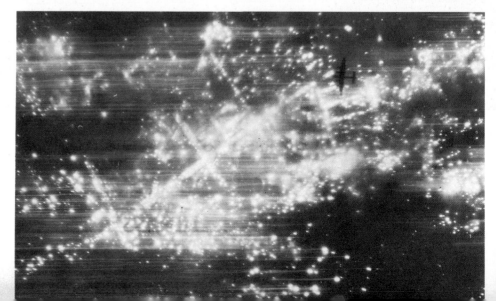

Despite their vast numerical inferiority the nightfighters, like their daytime colleagues, constantly return to the fray.

Yet in spite of the apparently hopeless situation, aircraft keep scoring new victories. The six pennants hoisted at IV./NJG 1's HQ in Schwansbelt Castle signal six further 'kills'.

Top: Major Schnaufer and his crew appear to be thrashing out a new tactic.
Below: Time to go: just one last look at the map.

218

Abschüsse der IV./N.J.G.1

Top: IV./NJG 1's victory table.
Below: This original document from the last days of the war speaks for itself. It lists victories and losses for NJG 1 from July 1940 to the end of hostilities. Section I shows victories, separated into day and night 'kills' for each Gruppe, and section II lists casualties in officers' and other ranks.

Erfolge u. Verluste

des Nachtjagdgeschwaders 1 in der Zeit vom
26. Juli 1940 bis Kriegsende

-.-.-.-.-.-.-.-.-.-.--.-.-.-.-

I.) A b s c h ü s s e :

	Tag :	Nacht :
Geschwaderstab	6	24
I./N.J.G. 1	–	585
II./N.J.G. 1	119	405
III./N.J.G. 1	7	343
IV./N.J.G. 1	13	816
Insgesamt :	145	2173

II.) V e r l u s t e :

	Offz.:	Uffz./Mansch.
Geschwaderstab	3	6
I./N.J.G. 1	35	118
II./N.J.G. 1	35	149
III./N.J.G. 1	33	154
IV./N.J.G. 1	29	114
Insgesamt :	135	541

Above: What was being celebrated? Those involved are, left to right, Drewes, Förster, Jabs, von Bonin, Schnaufer, Weissflog, Dobermann and Sutor.

Left: Drewes and his radio operator Oberfeldwebel Petz in serious discussion of a past mission. The fin of Hauptmann Drewes's Bf 110 bears the symbols of forty-seven victories.

Right: In this shot Drewes could be taken to symbolize a whole generation of young fighter pilots: daring, forthright and optimistic.

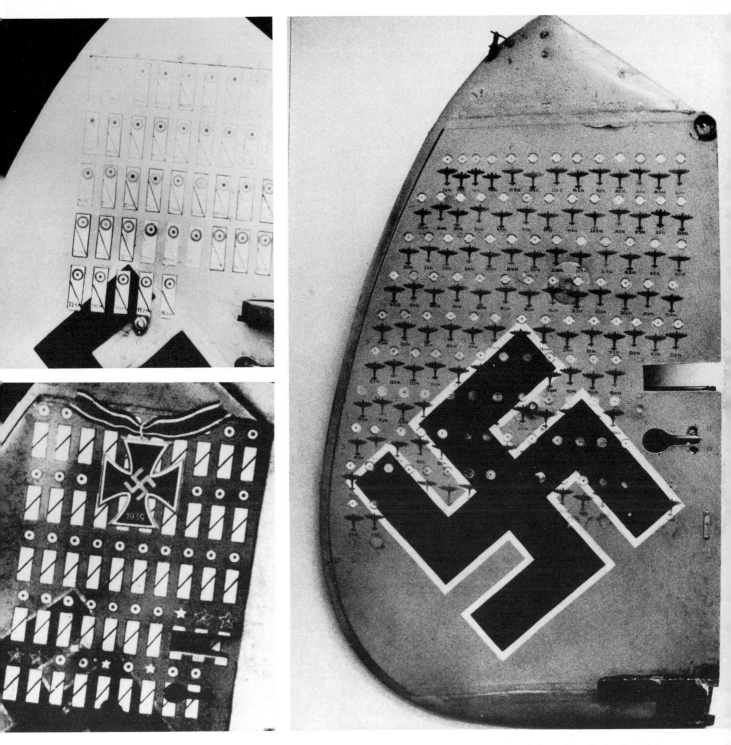

The time for great successes is past. From the beginning of 1945 the signs pointed increasingly to defeat. Even if the fins of the top nightfighters did testify to victorious days, they must inevitably succumb to the Allies' overwhelming air superiority. The fin on the right once belonged to Major Schnaufer's Bf 110G-4, and was photographed by the author in London's Imperial War Museum.

The End

The nightly battles in the skies over Germany were the last lap in an invisible race run in the design offices of aircraft and electronic factories in Germany, Britain and the USA. The men in the British and German aircraft were not just fliers and fighters, but also pioneers of a new technological era. In the field of radar technology the Germans allowed the initiative to slip steadily from their grasp in the course of the war. As late as 1942 the Allies had no equivalent to Würzburg, Freya or Lichtenstein, but then the British leapt ahead in the high-frequency field. (Translator's note: Britain, in fact, had the first airborne radar in 1940, but it was not very efficient because of its comparatively low frequency.)

From 1942 the nightfighter service was enlarged, but not until the middle of 1944 did the night Geschwader reach their full projected strength. Yet, although at their numerical peak, many units were grounded by the collapse of the control organization and by the fuel shortage. Another contributory factor in the cessation of German nightfighting activities was the aircraft themselves; the many former Zerstörer which had been converted into nightfighters and gradually improved in their new rôle, had fought an unequal battle from the beginning, and now finally went under. Even though the German nightfighter service had never been in a position to protect the towns and their inhabitants from the ever-increasing raids, the fact that victories were being scored right up to the end testifies in no uncertain manner to its determination.

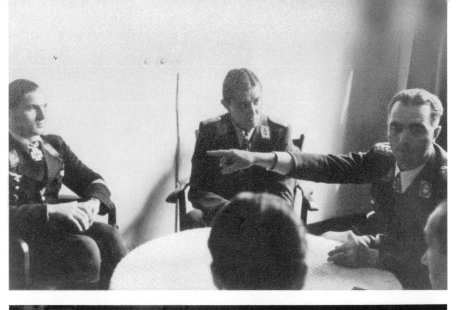

Top: Generalmajor Schmid seems to be pointing the way ahead. The sceptical faces of Hans-Joachim Jabs (centre) and Erich Weissflog (left) speak volumes.
Middle: Kommandeurs' conference. Generalmajor Galland, who has put aside all his decorations following his altercation with Göring, is surrounded by his officers; second from left is Oberst von Lossberg, who as an adviser on nightfighting to the Technical Bureau, was in large part responsible for the introduction of electronics into the field.
Below: The faces of Oberstleutnant Radusch, Kommodore of NJG 3 and Oberstleutnant Jabs of NJG 1 betray the general worry over the air-war situation at the end of 1944.

223

Left: Major Schnaufer converses with an engine mechanic. This Bf 110 has a straight flame-damping exhaust manifold.

Right: Schnaufer and radio operator Oberfeldwebel Gänseler chat with the technicians.

Opposite page, top: Schnaufer gives the ground crew a hand to push his Bf 110 into the hangar. This 110G-4 had two fixed upward-firing MG 151s in the rear cockpit.

Opposite page, below: Schnaufer, with 121 night victories to his credit in 'only' 164 operational sorties, was awarded the Diamonds to his Ritterkreuz on 16 October 1944. His crew, Leutnant Rumpelhardt and Oberfeldwebel Gänseler, are due a large part of the credit.

224

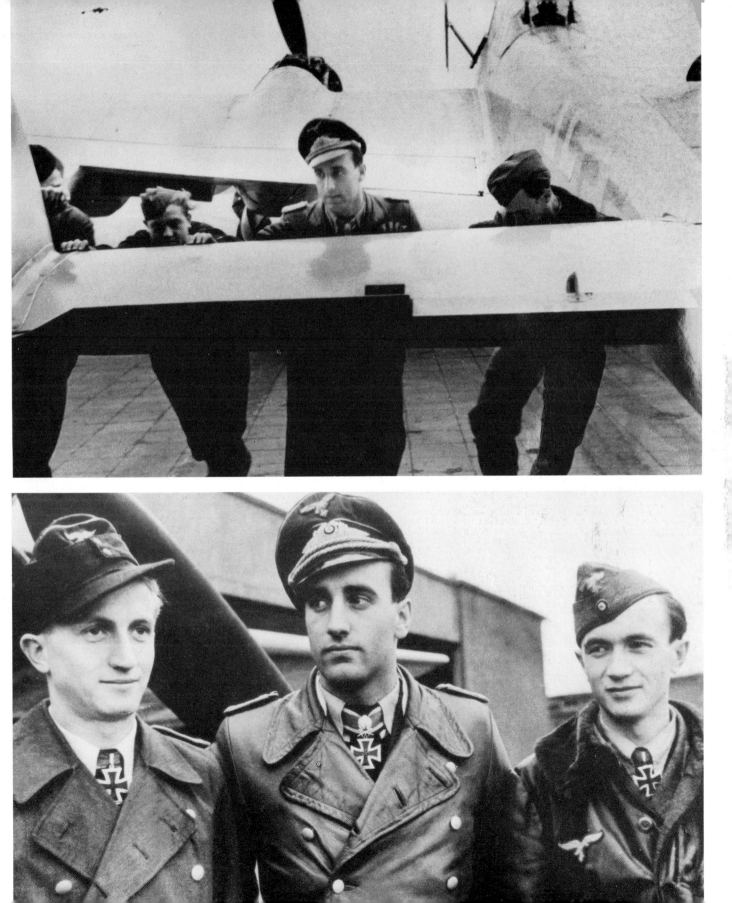

Left: Night after night whole districts in the cities go up in flames.
Right: The Bf 110G-4 flown by Hauptmann Wilhelm Johnen entered Swiss airspace while pursuing an American bomber formation on 28 April 1944, and was forced to land at Dübendorf near Zürich.
Below: A German aircraft destroyed on the ground by American fighter-bombers.

Top: On 5 October 1944 the German night-fighter command suffered a severe loss. Oberst Helmut Lent, Kommodore of NJG 3 and wearer of the Knight's Cross with Diamonds, crashed on landing at Paderborn in his Ju 88C-6. Lent was severely injured and died on 7 October. His radio operator Kubisch, Oberleutnant Klöss and a war reporter, Leutnant Kark also died with him.
Middle: Helmut Lent lies in state guarded by (left to right) his comrades Jabs, Schönert, Hadeball, Radusch and Streining.
Below: Hermann Göring salutes a great nightfighter pilot.

227

The funeral becomes a great demonstration of the worth and devotion to duty of Oberst Lent. His coffin is carried by paratroopers and escorted by Ritterkreuz-bearers. High-ranking officers and representatives of the Wehrmacht and State take part in the burial ceremony; third from left is Generalmajor Ibel, 3. Jagddivision, Generalmajor Schmid, Secretary of State Obergruppenführer Ahrens, General Wolf, II. Luftgau (Air District, ground organization). A chapter in aviation history comes to an end with the death of Helmut Lent.

228

The end of a tragic and bad time is at hand. Growing shortages of fuel and ammunition keep the nightfighters firmly on the ground. The Americans, marching in from the west and south, find lined-up at the sides of runways, or camouflaged in the woods, the remains of the once highly successful German nightfighters, now so much scrap metal.

Opposite page, left: The night-fighter Geschwader could do no more than their day fighter colleagues to stem the destruction of German cities.

Right: Oberst Falck, one of the founding fathers of the German night-fighter service, sits in the sun with an American interrogation officer.

Below: The victory parade of Patton's tanks is photographed by a few GIs from the wings of an He 219. The war is over.